Minnetonka Story

*The Onawa, world champion
first-class sloop — 1893*

Minnetonka Story

*A series of stories
covering Lake Minnetonka's years
from canoe to cruiser*
By
Blanche Nichols Wilson

THE COLWELL PRESS, INC · MINNEAPOLIS, MINNESOTA · 1950

To my children
         whose lively interest in stories
about their lake prompted me
                 to write this book.

Aт тне close of the first World War we exchanged our Minneapolis property for Deephaven acres. Everything on our new place needed attention. Our SOS brought older men from Mound, Wayzata and Excelsior pinch hitting for the boys still in the service.

Those men arrived early one morning while I was feeding the chickens. I could hear laughing and talking, and then, as though coming down from the sky, the full, rich strains of an aria from "Die Meistersinger."

From behind the lilacs I could see what was going on. One of the men astride the ridgepole examining the chimney was singing with all his might. Such singing I had never heard off the stage! Forty years before, that songster on our roof had sung in Chicago and San Francisco grand opera, taking summer jobs as tenor soloist on Lake Minnetonka's big boats.

That first day stories about "way back when" came thick and fast. The next day—still more talk and considerably less work. It was then I drove a hard bargain. If they would keep their stories till noon—so that our children from school could enjoy them too—I would serve a hot lunch for all of us together.

Immediately the tempo of work quickened to an amazing degree. Then at lunch time Minnetonka's early history passed before us in grand parade. As soon as our entertainers had finished their work and gone, my children asked me to write down those stories and all the others I could gather.

Interviews with Minnetonkans, those living here and those who had moved away, have furnished the bulk of this material.

Preface

To talk to the old settlers was the privilege of a lifetime, whether they were on crutches, in wheel chairs, in bed for life, or still able to get about. Without exception, they became interested friends when they knew why I had come. They were proud to tell of their pioneer experiences.

In homes where the early settlers had passed on, their gray-haired children shared with me the pioneer stories "pa and ma used to tell." Often they brought out old keepsakes, albums, candlesticks—once even an old silk hat and its companion, a modest bonnet. Before those mute witnesses of the past they talked and I listened.

To learn of Minnetonka's reputation as a pleasure resort was an easy and delightful task, simply because a great many still living around the lake have a vivid remembrance of Minnetonka's golden days which faded with the turn of the century. In the South I found still others who recall with pleasure the highlights of Minnetonka's hospitality which outrivalled that of other watering places of those days.

To write about events known to one's neighbors; in fact, to write about one's neighbors themselves is not an easy task. After completing each unit about an individual, I read it to the person himself or his nearest of kin, correcting where necessary.

This simple narration of life around Lake Minnetonka is, I realize, far too scant to cover the subject. Friends on all sides have been patient and painstaking in supplying accurate information. To them I am exceedingly grateful.

BLANCHE NICHOLS WILSON

..... | *Contents*

Contents

Frontispiece. The *Onawa*, world champion first-class sloop, owned by Ward C. Burton and Hazen Burton and sailed by the Burtons, A. M. Shuck, and Arthur Dyer, 1893.

Illustrations follow page 158

Illustrations

Minnetonka Story

| CHAPTER I | *Who Discovered Lake Minnetonka?* |

T_{HE} March sun was warm and friendly—favorable weather for building. Wayzata's first two log houses had gone up like "greased lightning." Their owners stopped long enough to give their work the once-over.

"Be done by tonight, won't we? How about bringing the wives out tomorrow?" queried the older man.

A shadow crossed his companion's handsome face. "That's what's been bothering me all day. Has a man any right to pick up his wife and plunk her down in the middle of this blasted bunch of jibbering redskins? What's to hinder 'em from giving us hell any minute?"

"There's your answer, brother, sitting over there in front of her wigwam. Say, why don't *we* take a little rest, too?"

The two men sat down, sociably sharing the same enormous stump. "Plenty of room left for that old squaw over there," observed the younger man with a grin.

"Oh, I was just going to say that old Manitoucha there is the answer to the question you just asked. Let me tell you, son, that as long as she lives, not a drop of blood will be shed around this lake."

The young pioneer was skeptical. "How can you be sure of that?"

"It's this way, old Manitoucha explained it all to me the other day—"

"Wait a minute," interrupted the younger man. "Here's some 'toback'. I can listen better while we smoke. All ready now."

"Good idea. Thanks. Well, according to her this lake is sacred to the Great Manitou who loves peace. Thousands of moons ago he gave Minnetonka to the Sioux on the promise never to defile its shores by bloodshed. Old Manitoucha's got Chief Little Six—he's her foster son—and all this tribe right under her thumb. She keeps reminding her people of the curse waiting for those who forget."

"Sounds good. What's the curse?" asked the listener.

"Oh, she calls it the curse of the rolling head."

* * *

Old Manitoucha sat watching the pale faces finish their cabins. "More will come," she muttered, "but what must be, must be."

That had been her father's philosophy. Her father, a great man, chief of the medicine men on Enchanted Island! Good that he had gone to the Happy Hunting Ground still tasting the glory of his tribe. Had not the Sioux, the Manitou's chosen people, been called out of the Valley of Creation and promised "the pleasantest place on earth" if they could find it?

How her father's eyes had glowed when he told of the ceaseless wanderings of his tribesmen. At last they entered a noble forest. Fruit hung from the trees. Berries glistened at their feet. Deer were fat, game birds heavy.

Beyond lay "big water," beautiful as a lovely woman wearing islands like emeralds upon her breast, and flinging her arms far back among the hills as though looking for something warm and human to embrace.

"This is it," the wanderers whispered in awe, "this is it, our promised land."

In gratitude to the Great Spirit, the Sioux vowed before their god Manitou that no bloodshed should ever violate the sanctity of this land. The curse of the rolling head was in store for anyone who might forget that early vow.

Every seventh moon her father had explained this curse to his tribesmen: "Head roll, by sun, by moon. Head tired? No rest. Head thirsty? No drink. Head hungry? No eat. Head afraid? No legs, no run. Head love? No arms, no hands to catch pretty one. Head roll, no stop—roll, roll—no head left."

Some years later old Manitoucha sat again in the sun. She

4

never got tired of counting the new log cabins springing up along the shore or of noticing how many little white children were coming to live by her lake. Pale face and redskin had remained at peace. The thought sent a smile of satisfaction through Manitoucha's wrinkles, a smile that attracted a group of children loitering nearby in the hope of a little maple sugar and maybe even a story.

That day Manitoucha told them about a wild-turkey feast on the shores of Minnetonka hundreds of moons ago. She showed how carefully the squaws had to turn their fowls on spits to keep them from falling into the fire, and how little salt each fowl could have—only three pinches apiece, salt was that scarce!

Then throwing off her heavy blanket, old Manitoucha did the turkey dance to show how the young braves danced to pack down their overload of turkey meat. It was a wild, tempestuous dance, and it worked. The young braves always came back for still more turkey.

Suddenly—and here old Manitoucha laid aside gayety and became dramatic—suddenly in the midst of that long-ago feast, the chief raised his bow and arrow. Every brave did likewise. There was deathly silence. Someone was approaching. The bushes parted. There stood the first "pale faces" the red men had ever seen.

There were only three white men. The leader was in black blankets that hung from his shoulders. On his breast was a shining thing: "The Cross," he said, laying one hand on the gleaming emblem and pointing to the sky with the other. He seemed exhausted. When he swayed unsteadily, his attendants hurried to his side and eased him down to a bed of grass.

After eating much juicy turkey meat, the pale face was strong enough to explain how the Great Spirit had once lived here on earth, healing and blessing and teaching people to live in peace. But in spite of all He did, He met His death upon the Cross. Again the priest touched the shining thing on his breast. Then stretching his arms out over the moonlit water—and here Manitoucha solemnly arose and made a similar gesture—the priest said many more strange things. His face shone with kindness. Finally, he and his companions stretched out on the shore and went to sleep.

Long that night the whole tribe sat silently watching the fire—thinking, wondering. Where had the pale faces come from? Why were they sleeping so quietly, so entirely without fear? Was the Great Spirit watching over them?

In the morning a heavy rain was falling; the three visitors had disappeared. At this point Manitoucha rose to conclude her story: "Father Hennepin, first pale face see our lake. Great white priest show our people Cross, point to Great Spirit."

* * *

Father Hennepin *should* have discovered Minnetonka. The truth is he never saw our lake, Manitoucha's story to the contrary. An idealist with his head full of visions and his tongue full of poetry should have been assigned by the immortal gods to make the discovery of this queen of lakes nestled in the lap of luxuriant forests—this friendly, sociable beauty, fickle as a flirt and lovely as a dream.

Cultured, refined, a lover of art, Father Hennepin would have appreciated the high quality of Minnetonka's beauty. But the great priest did not come this way even though our lake belonged to the French Empire at that time.

When Louis XIV wanted to know how much land he had in the Louisiana Territory west of the Mississippi, he sent La Salle to explore that river and find its source. Father Hennepin, Franciscan Missionary of the Recollect Order, came with La Salle to convert the Indians. At the Illinois River, La Salle turned back to Canada and sent Father Hennepin with two attendants to explore the Mississippi.

Father Hennepin canoed up the Mississippi, in 1683, to the falls which he christened St. Anthony of Padua. At the falls he was taken captive by a band of Sioux Indians who started north with their three white prisoners. After traveling for "a distance of sixty leagues," they finally reached that part of Minnesota abounding in lakes. "Mille Lacs! a thousand lakes!" cried Father Hennepin. The largest lake of the region seemed later to appropriate this name to itself, and to this day we call just one lake a thousand, Mille Lacs.

Upon his arrival at Mille Lacs, Father Hennepin found the Sioux engaged in a wild-turkey feast that lasted many, many days. Given their freedom several weeks later, the priest and his comrades came back to St. Anthony Falls, staying close to the Mississippi until their return to Canada by way of the Illinois River and the Great Lakes.

And so it happened that prosaic Mille Lacs was discovered and named by the priest who should have come to Minnetonka instead. The Sioux Indians here evidently had borrowed from their kinsmen around Mille Lacs this story of Father Hennepin's visit and had given it a Minnetonka setting.

Old Manitoucha would have been grieved to know that her story did not belong to Minnetonka at all. She would have been surprised that a little pale face, listening to her story that day, could recall every detail of it at our lunch table sixty years afterwards.

* * *

For nearly a hundred and fifty years after Father Hennepin's contribution to Minnesota history, Minnetonka lay undisturbed. One bright morning in the summer of 1822, the inquisitive eyes of two fourteen-year-old boys rested upon a lake never before seen by white men. After all, perhaps this was the way for Minnetonka to be discovered. Youth with its dreams and its future is no doubt nearer Nature's heart than maturity with its experiences and its past.

Those boys were an interesting pair. Joe Brown was a runaway drummer boy always seeking adventure. Joe had already made valuable explorations along the Mississippi and was on the lookout for new worlds.

Will Snelling, son of Colonel Snelling, had a yen for adventure too. Accustomed to strict army discipline, he was attracted to the undisciplined, venturesome Joe. One day the boys took "French leave" of the fort and canoed up a creek* to the lake which was its source. They fastened their canoe and made their

*Later known as Brown's River, Little Falls Creek, and finally Minnehaha Creek.

way slowly along the wooded vine-draped shore of this "inland sea abounding in islands and peninsulas." With hats full of strawberries they sat down to watch a mother deer play with her fawn. It was a scene of perfect peace.

At Fort Snelling, however, things were far from peaceful. What had become of the two? Why had they not returned before dark? Something terrible must have happened to them. Had they fallen prey to hostile red men?

After an anxious night for everybody at the fort, detachments of soldiers were sent in search of the boys. By evening they were found feasting upon fried fish and strawberries.

The story goes that "Papa" Snelling was so enraged over the whole thing that he forbade any mention of the escapade. But in the record books of Fort Snelling an entry was made to the effect that in the year 1822, two boys, Joe Brown and Will Snelling, made the discovery of a large lake still in the possession of the Sioux Indians and lying to the southwest of St. Anthony Falls. In deference to Colonel Snelling the matter was discreetly hushed up, and Lake Minnetonka fell back into oblivion.

CHAPTER II | *"She Sleeps,*
My Lady Sleeps"

For thirty years after her discovery in 1822 by a couple of adventurous boys, Sioux-owned and Sioux-loved Minnetonka slept in peace on the very doorstep of the white man's world. While Minnesota was busy making history all around her, Minnetonka napped on, undisturbed by the white man's fuss and flurry.

For those thirty years more Minnetonka's red children trod her shores with moccasined feet or gracefully plied her waters with canoe and paddle. Indian life continued to follow its age-old conservation pattern: enough game and fish for food; enough pelts and skins for clothing; enough porcupine quills for ornament; "down wood" for fire; crowded saplings for tent poles.

While Minnetonka slumbered on in the lap of the Big Woods, thousands of wild things suddenly awoke to approaching danger —the white settlers were coming. Tumbling headlong into this nearby sanctuary, all sorts of terrified creatures found safety.

During her long nap Minnetonka did not dream that at one time she was in Michigan, in Iowa, and then in Wisconsin. Minnesota, with no identity of her own, took turns at staying with these neighbors.

While Minnesota was still a part of Wisconsin, H. H. Sibley, the talented, farsighted manager of the American Fur Company at Mendota, was sent to Washington as a Wisconsin delegate. He proposed to Congress that Wisconsin should split up and allow Minnesota to become a territory of the United States Government, like Wisconsin herself.

Congress favored Mr. Sibley's proposal, advising the people of Wisconsin to convene immediately to decide upon their western boundary. Strange suggestions were made in that convention. One greedy Wisconsinite proposed that this boundary line be drawn north and south a dozen miles west of the Rum River. Such a decision would have meant Wisconsin around Lake Minnetonka instead of Minnesota.

In 1849, as soon as the St. Croix and the Mississippi were declared our eastern boundary, Minnesota became a territory. Trim enough on the east, Minnesota on the west sprawled back to the Missouri River.

Just a dozen years before Minnesota became a territory, the settlement of St. Paul had begun to grow out of a whisky jug. Mark Twain piloted his steamboat up the Mississippi to St. Paul to have a look at the town. His comment was this:

"How solemn and beautiful is the thought that the earliest pioneer of civilization is never the steamboat, never the railroad, never the Sabbath school, never the missionary — but always — whisky. This great vanguard arrived upon the ground which St. Paul now occupies in June, 1837. Yes, at that date Pierre Parrant built his first cabin, uncorked his jug and began to sell whisky to the Indians. The result is before us!"

Pierre Parrant proved a good businessman; more grog shops, more whisky. "Pig's Eye" was the first name of this sorry little hamlet whose tipsy shanties clung to the hillsides, desperately afraid of falling into the river. All unlovely was this wretched white settlement, unlovely even in name. Not many miles away, in peaceful purity, lovely Minnetonka still slept on, guarded as jealously by her Sioux admirers as the Sleeping Beauty of the fairy tale.

One day a missionary changed the name Pig's Eye to St. Paul, and the settlement began to thrive. In spite of its poor start St. Paul had within it an element of growth, a strategic location for river traffic. It had hopes and ambitions besides. And now, the governor was coming. All St. Paul's "three hundred souls" turned out to welcome him. Pride and satisfaction shone on every face. No longer were they sheep without a shepherd.

As the governor's steamboat came into sight, some ill-starred mortal asked: "Where is the governor going to put up?" This withering question passed like wildfire through the little crowd. Everybody knew that every cabin, every shanty in the settlement was already full to capacity. It was one thing to have a governor; but where to put him was the question.

While the steamboat was docking, a tall handsome gentleman of gracious countenance strode through the crowd. "How're ye, Sibley?" "Howdy, Mr. Sibley?" With friendly dignity this man returned their greetings, but hastened on to welcome the new territorial governor, Alexander Ramsey. With singular grace and ease, he presented to the people their new magistrate.

As soon as the applause permitted, Mr. Sibley announced: "For the present, Governor Ramsey will stay at my place. Call on him there." A sigh of relief and a new storm of applause greeted this announcement. To this day, Governor Alexander Ramsey's desk stands in the Sibley House, a monument to their David-Jonathan friendship which lasted through life.

Meanwhile St. Paul's twin was stirring into life. Minneapolis had two fathers, both highly respectable men. Franklin Steele was a sober-minded man of unusual insight and business ability. In the whirling waters of St. Anthony Falls he saw "worlds of power" which he proceeded to harness to sawmill and flour mill. Result: the settlement of St. Anthony. Colonel John Stevens fostered the growth of a little village on his own claim and built a home on the river bank across from the present Great Northern station. His little village was called Minneapolis.

Both fathers of these new settlements were men of education, refinement and discernment. Each was proud of his own village, its government and its institutions. Finally, in 1872, these rival settlements merged under the name Minneapolis.

At last Minnesota was a territory with a governor and a legislature. A site was chosen for our great university. School lands were set aside in the counties that were being laid out. The state penitentiary was located at Stillwater. St. Paul was chosen as the state capital. The twin cities had started to grow. Industry and commerce were on the increase. The newly established St. Anthony *Express* sounded this optimistic note: "Every successive steamboat arrival in St. Paul pours out on the landing men big with hope, anxious to do something to mould the future of the new state."

Minnesota itself was wide awake, but not a sound of all this throbbing new life had come to the ears of sleeping Minnetonka. She continued undisturbed, untroubled, while only a few miles away whole caravans of covered wagons were passing the Sibley home.

"These settlers must have more room!" exclaimed Governor Ramsey to his host. "What's to be done about it, Sibley?"

The governor's friend and adviser answered with a directness that led to the final solution of the matter. "Well, nine-tenths of Minnesota is still in the hands of the Indians. Something must be done, I agree, and as soon as possible. A treaty with the redskins might open up a lot of this land to the whites."

The result of this conversation was a treaty with the Sioux. According to one of Minnesota's historians: "The most important measure of the year 1851 was the treaty with the Dahkotahs (Sioux) by which the west side of the Mississippi and the valley of the Minnesota River were opened up to the hardy immigrant."

This is where Minnetonka comes into the picture—"west of the Mississippi." In return for the immense tract of land indicated in the "Traverse Treaty des Sioux and Mendota," the Federal Government promised to pay the Sioux the sum of $3,000,000. But Dr. W. W. Folwell says, in his *History of Minnesota*, that the first payment of $30,000 was practically all that ever came to the red man in exchange for this great stretch of country. He further adds that most of this $30,000 was soon back in the white man's pocket in return for trinkets and "fire water."

In 1852, precisely thirty years after Minnetonka had been discovered, Congress ratified the Traverse Treaty. For the lake, this treaty was the kiss that woke the Sleeping Beauty—it meant wake up, Minnetonka!

CHAPTER III | *"Awake, My Lake!"*

W<small>HEN</small> a Boston friend heard that we were living in Deephaven, she hastened to write: "Can it be that you are so near the lake we call 'Uncle Hezekiah's lake'? You'll know why we named it that when you read this letter of his, the last he ever wrote us. It tells so much about your lake, I know you'll love it.

"Uncle Hezekiah was really our great uncle, Grandpa Hotchkiss' oldest brother. Now, why in the name of sense didn't all the Hotchkisses go west when Uncle Hezekiah wanted them to? If they had, I might be a neighbor of yours right now! Here is a copy of his letter."

"My Lake, Minnesota Terr.
Oct. 12, 1852

"Hello folks!

"How would you like to exchange Boston for Paradise? I wouldn't trade my log cabin for all the mansions of the 'Hub'; or my sapphire lake for the whole Atlantic. Governor Ramsey has just named my lake Minnetonka, the Sioux jargon for 'big water.'

"You folks wouldn't know me after all these years of trapping with the Indians. I'm pretty nigh a Sioux myself, dress like 'em, act like 'em, eat like 'em, canoe and hunt and fish like 'em; their way is best. I'm the only pale face around this lake. I'm never uneasy with them, but I do get deathly sick of their hellish jibberish, it gets on my nerves, and their war whoops still give me the ague.

"'Fire water' turns these redskins into demons. I see real drunk Indians only when I go into the white settlements — St. Paul's thick with 'em. You children can find St. Paul on the map; it's the capital of Minnesota Territory now.

"These red fellows are going to have to clear out as soon as the Traverse Treaty des Sioux and Mendota is ratified by Congress this winter, and that's just what's bothering me. You've read about this new Indian treaty, I reckon, in the Boston *Transcript*.

13

Minnetonka Story

"Yesterday I heard the crack of rifles way off in the woods, and awhile back when I was canoeing along by the outlet of My Lake, I heard the blow of axes. Somebody on shore was laughing fit to split. (Indians don't laugh.) Now, what does all this mean? Just one thing — the whites are coming.

"Didn't sleep very sound last night thinking how My Lake's got to wake up and live in the white man's world. So, to pass the time away, I made up a whacking good piece of poetry; this morning, plague on it, can't remember a blessed line of it except the title, 'Awake, My Lake!' Good start anyhow, don't you think?

"When the shake-up comes, I'll surely miss my good trusty Feather-in-the-Face. 'Friday,' I call him for short. All this time I've felt safe with him near. Hope I'm right, but I feel sure that he'd warn me if there was any mischief on foot.

"Pretty soon, I'll have to give up trapping and take to the soil. I'm here ahead of the game you see, I've made my choice of a claim. Now why don't all of you pack up and come west next spring on the run? I'd stake out a claim for every single one of you. Nobody here yet. Wait, I've got to take that back.

"There is one fellow miles below, on the outlet — where I heard the chopping the other day. I've found out he's waiting to put up a sawmill as soon as he can file on the spot where the water power looks best. And the other day, come to remember, Friday and I were canoeing along the southeast shore when we caught sight of a man stepping off land and stopping to drive stakes now and then. Bet he's got some folks down East, too.

"My house? Well, you should see it balancing like the Tower of Pisa, high up on a point of land. Why, if I were a 'lazy bones,' I could lie a-bed and fish out of the window. Fresh-water fish, none of your mackerel or haddy! Of course, you'd miss clams and oysters; they don't grow here. But what would you think of a new kind of waterfowl for dinner every day? Sometimes, I prefer grouse or pheasant; they're so juicy it's hard to keep your chin clean.

"Yesterday a prairie chicken came up to my doorstep. I kept still as a mouse and he walked away. Soon a quail looked in on me. Both are excellent eating, but my idea of hospitality made me let both of them depart in peace. Queer, these are prairie birds that don't generally like heavy woods. Just the other day I stumbled onto a covey of quail while out walking with Pedro.

"Pedro, children, is my pet fawn. He is such a graceful thing! Lots of company — why, he follows me everywhere. The minute I sit down, there's his head in my lap. One day last spring I found him, a wee bit of a fellow, all cold and hungry. I befriended him and brought him up against great odds. He'll be deserting me one of these days. Just let some flirtatious young doe come along – he'll leave me without a tear.

"Oh well, such is life! Big herds of deer come to drink in the cove a few rods up shore, but Pedro hasn't let on to see them yet. I hope he'll stay by me this winter. It'll be hard enough to give him up next spring.

"Last week a squaw brought me a bowl of maple sugar. Now don't you girls turn up your nose, wondering if it's clean. All I can say is that it suits me first rate – best I ever tasted. I'm planning to make some maple sugar myself next spring. I've got the trees right here in my yard. I'll have it all made when you folks get here.

"You'd better come out here and see My Lake for yourselves. You can't imagine how she glows in the sunshine and glitters in the moonlight. On grey days, she looks sad and lonely, just like I feel sometimes, but in no time at all, she can kick up her heels and treat you to a first-class squall. Yes, sir, she's tricky all right, but I'm never leaving her, never!

"You never saw such country as this around here. All sorts of small fruit grow wild here. Raspberries, strawberries, gooseberries covered with long spikes – you don't notice 'em though when they're cooked – the spikes I mean. Cherries, grapes, hazelnuts, plenty everywhere. Just made grape jell, Friday packed the sugar home on his back from St. Paul.

"Birds? Well, I never saw the beat of the birds, and the way they sing is enough to make you wish for cotton in your ears. You'll like everything around here – you can't help it – no place like it!

"Come on out next spring! If I knew you were coming bag and baggage, I'd have something to plan for all winter. I get blue as a whetstone when I think how different things are going to be next year. Let me hear from you soon!

"Please do come; you'll never regret the move.

Your hopeful
UNCLE HEZEKIAH.'

CHAPTER IV

The First White Woman
Sees Lake Minnetonka

ONE August day in 1852, Fort Snelling had a pleasant surprise. A gay little party of New Yorkers arrived to have a look at the Fort and the nearby settlements of St. Anthony and St. Paul. The moving spirit of this group was Mrs. W. H. Ellet, talented wife of a professor of chemistry at Columbia University. Already a writer of established reputation, she was now looking for new material in the Minnesota Territory.

Near the Fort was an Indian trading post. Every day squaws trotted in with their strawberries and maple sugar and braves flung their fish and venison upon the counter demanding "toback." "Where come from, where?" Mrs. Ellet's question was met with a shrug or a grunt until one day an old squaw mumbled, "Big water." At last, a clue!

Following this lead, Mrs. Ellet began to unearth what little was known about this mysterious lake referred to as "Peninsula Lake" until recently christened "Minnetonka" by Governor Ramsey. She learned that several parties of men had been fishing and hunting out that way and that earlier in the spring a couple of serious-minded businessmen had explored the lake and had found a mill site a few miles down its outlet.

She was told that eagles built on the rocky shores of the Upper Lake and that they hardly stirred from their nests when one reached under them for eggs—they had not yet learned to fear humans. A young doctor from St. Louis showed her his scalp-dance stone the size of a human head. He had found it on a high promontory, Spirit Knob on Breezy Point, overlooking the lake. Around this stone piled high with the scalps of their victims,

16

warriors used to perform ceremonial dances in honor of the Great Manitou. The yellow spots on the red stone denoted the number of warriors taking part in the dance.

Mrs. Ellet decided that Lake Minnetonka was worth seeing. She planned to make the trip the next day. At this, the gentlemen of her acquaintance voiced their alarm. "Impossible, it's too hard a trip for a woman!"

In spite of their warning, Mrs. Ellet hurried over to St. Anthony, where she found "co-operators" enough to make a sizeable party. They secured a team, a driver, and a strong, light wagon. All that was left to make the venture a success was a supply of "comforters," blankets, and food enough to last until the next day.

After leaving the settlement of St. Anthony, Mrs. Ellet's party took the road over the prairie to Lake Calhoun and struck an old Indian trail which led through scrub-oak country relieved here and there by clumps of birch, maple, and white oak.

In Mrs. Ellet's "Summer Rambles in the West," she described her trip to Minnetonka. ". . . We were treading ground to which the white man's claim had never reached as yet, over which the Indian had held sway from a period beyond the memory of tradition. Now and then we came upon an old camping ground where were still visible the traces of their fires, and where the poles over which the Sioux lodges are built were still standing.

"On we went skirting marshes and climbing ridges, on and on, as before, till the welcome sight of a broad bright stream rushing along with a current 'fiercely glad' made us aware that we were approaching the termination of our drive. We could see it afar, winding and flashing through the meadow, with its clustering bushes dipping their branches into its clear, deep water.

" 'Little Falls Creek,' said our guide in answer to our question what was its name, and we recognized the same lovely stream [Minnehaha Creek] we had marvelled at on our way to Fort Snelling and its bewitching leap at the Falls [Minnehaha Falls].* We forded this rapid outlet and plowed our way through a forest of undergrowth along the margin of a broad meadow and came

*So named after Longfellow's poem "Hiawatha" was published in 1855.

into full view of a haystack, the hermit's hay, we were informed. The hermit chanced to be absent from home, but Mr. S. living in the hermit's lodge welcomed us with much courtesy.

"The basket was unpacked meanwhile and a hasty lunch taken, for we had several miles further to go. Those who were bent on fishing made their preparations and leaving our luggage in the wagon and fastening the horses, we took the footpath to the landing place just on the bend of the stream. Presently the whole party was seated in the boat, paddling up the swift deep outlet.

"The water is from two to six feet or more deep, and would serve for steamboat navigation. A small steamer is talked of for another season, and a mill for which Mr. Simon Stevens was then hauling logs.

"The waters were so clear we could often see the sandy bottom, and numbers of fish sporting around us. The white and yellow water lilies grew profusely near the banks which were now marshy, now rising to an elevated ridge of oak land. Then we entered the woods where the uplands rose to considerable elevation. A long peninsula was rounded, and about four miles from the shanty, we found ourselves in a clear and beautiful lake, the eastern arm, the first, in the chain we were entering.

"The bright sheet was nearly circular, and a mile across in any direction. As we shot over its unruffled surface, we asked each other what name should be given to this first brilliant in the garland of gems; and claiming the right, as the first white woman who had ever looked on its beauty, to bestow a name in compliment to the English portion of our party we called it Lake Browning [Gray's Bay], after the great poetess. Portions of this lake, near the shores, are covered with wild rice, rushes, and water lilies. . . .

"Passing through a narrow strait, we then entered the second lake, rounding a sharp point and started with surprise at the picture which unexpectedly presented itself. A noble sheet of water, nearly three miles in width and three and a half long lay embraced by lofty bluffs, not rocky but rising almost perpendicularly from the pebbly shores, densely wooded nearly to the water's edge, and having their ridges and summits covered with tall, heavy timber. Some distance back of these extends a fine prairie. Two bold headlands, about midway up, stretched far out into the lake, and at our left the loveliest cove in the world, with a beach of white sand and pebbles, was pointed out as a splendid fishing ground. Two of the men landed here with all necessary apparatus for making havoc among the finny tribes. But first with due formality and reverently standing, we gave to the lake the name I had chosen—Lake Bryant [Wayzata Bay]— and read aloud a few lines from the poet appropriate to the scene.

"It was on this lake that a deer was speared in the water by the first party of visitors, while the creature was swimming across. Deer and other game abound, it is said, in these woods; and wild birds that build on inaccessible heights have their nests in the boughs of these lofty cedars. We saw one noble eagle poised on the wing over our heads, and looking down as if in wonder at our invasion of his home. On the beach agates and cornelians may be picked up in abundance, and one of fine quality which I brought away will make, when cut, a beautiful memorial of the locality.

"An extremely narrow isthmus connects Lake Bryant with the third lake. We landed and climbed over ragged prominences and fallen cedars, the steep promontory dividing their waters, and having gained a height of some sixty feet gazed upon the scene before us with emotions of wonder and admiration. The lofty headland is half a mile in length, running out from the southern shore of the lake, and for some distance from the point is not more than two rods in width. . . .

"The signs of Dakota worship show indubitably that this place was holy ground. The appearance of the ground; the marks upon the trees; the ruins of rude altars; the remnants of old scalp-hoops; the painted stones, and all such implements of savage rites, prove this theory correct.

"The view from this point up the lake was a magnificent one, partaking of grandeur in no small degree; for the fresh breeze, which had not full play on the other lakes, here lifted the waves into billows and flung them on the beach at our feet. . . . Far as the eye could reach stretched the blue, sparkling waters, sprinkled here and there with islands thickly wooded and bordered with a deep dark forest [the Big Woods] wholly unlike the woods on the uplands, for the trees were of great height and size.

"The timber was chiefly of oak and elm of different kinds, white oak, sugar maple, hickory, poplar, cottonwood with a few evergreens. Long and narrow peninsulas from either shore, rising into promontories of startling abruptness and height, projected miles into the lake, some not more than twenty feet wide, forming beautiful bays, in which, they say, fish are in marvelous abundance. Two small islands lay just before us, tufted with thick green foliage, and midway up the lake, a large and beautiful one, embracing, it is said, 1,000 acres; a place resorted to by the Indians for making sugar.*

"The fourth lake [Upper Lake] is the largest in the chain. . . . It is said to have the finest scenery and to be walled by rocky, precipitous cliffs towering to a considerable height; but we could not have judged of this without sailing a number of miles past the headlands whose blue outline formed the limit of our view. This fourth lake has also a branch lying northward, and is said to contain ten islands of considerable size. A narrow stream connects it with a fifth and much smaller lake, and westward of this the others follow in succession.

"Colonel John Stevens* said the number in the chain was sixteen, as he had ascertained by actual exploration, and that the last lake approached within a few miles of the Minnesota River. The whole range runs nearly east and west.

"Mr. S., who accompanied us, informed me that in the beginning of the month he and a friend had found canoes in a cove beyond the farthest point in the third lake, and a well-marked Indian trail leading westward. They followed the trail; starting at seven in the morning, and after a walk of a few hours

*Big Island with an area of between 250 and 300 acres, according to Mr. Herbert Morse of Excelsior, was preempted by his father in 1855.
*Among the Colonel's descendants is Mrs. Charles S. Pillsbury (née Winston), Wayzata.

arrived at 'Little Six' [Shakopee], a Sioux village on the Minnesota. Dining there, they returned in the afternoon to the lake.

"On the shore of this third lake a location [Excelsior] has been chosen, and claims set up for a hundred families who are to remove thither next year. In some remote places we saw these claims designated by mere slips of board nailed against a tree.

"We felt no surprise to hear that this charming region had been so valued by the Dakotas as a hunting and fishing ground that they were said to have kept the knowledge of it from the white population as long as possible, and petitioned the governor for a reservation of territory which would have included this favorite possession. They loved this beautiful land, its clear water and deep forests; their ancient hunting ground, and the scene . . . of their sacrifices. There is reason, indeed, to suppose that they came yearly from great distances to make offerings to their deities thereabouts. But the rapacity of the white man denied them this beloved retreat, and immigrants already press in to occupy the country of the receding race. A year or two more will banish their canoes from these waters and show the majestic headlands sprinkled with clearings and germs of settlements."

| CHAPTER V | *Five Little Towns and How They Grew* |

Part I – SHORE SETTLEMENTS

"Towns will spring up," prophesied an early pioneer writer —and they did. The first five shore settlements differed from each other as children in the same family are apt to do, and even with better right. To be sure they all had the same environment, the lake itself, but each had a vastly different heredity.

Minnetonka Mills started life with a rough-hewn sawmill. Excelsior was born in New York City on a piece of paper. Wayzata came into existence right in the center of Chief Shakopee's Indian village. Mound was born among the dead, asleep for ages in strange burial mounds. St. Albans nestled on the warm shoulder of sunny St. Albans Bay.

MINNETONKA MILLS

The casual stranger today is perplexed by the name, Minnetonka Mills. He looks in vain for the mills and the lake. It is hard for him to believe that this settlement was once a milling center, a shipping port on Lake Minnetonka, and a rival of Minneapolis as an industrial center.

The story of its early days begins with two men of imagination and common sense: Simon Stevens, brother of Colonel John Stevens, and Calvin Tuttle, the first treasurer of the Minnesota Territory. Together they explored this Sioux lake early in April, 1852, a whole year before the region was opened to white settlement.

Noting the gradual fall of the lake's swift outflowing stream, they chose the most favorable spot for the erection of a sawmill and drove stakes for adjacent claims. Almost at that same moment another "early bird" was choosing his claim not far from where

22

the Groveland School now stands. This man was James Shaver,* builder and carpenter, who was given the contract for building the new mill.

Stevens and Tuttle, feeling the weight of their project, invited Webster, Hollister and Atwood to join them. The moment word came that Congress had ratified the Traverse Treaty, this new company of five members petitioned the territorial legislature for dam rights, which were granted. Immediately they threw a twelve-foot dam across the stream, nearly opposite the spot where the Burwell School stands today.

Finally, on May 12, 1853, dam and mill stood ready for business, the second sawmill built west of the Mississippi. The new dam furnished the necessary water power, creating at the same time a deep, broad shipping channel from mill to lake. Thus Minnetonka Mills, milling center and lake port, was brought into existence.

These are the cold facts of the business end of the matter, but for romance and human interest we must turn to James Shaver and his wife Sarah. A right smart sort she was, with a head full of curls and common sense.

Few young married women are called upon from the first to try to please a dozen men—one is usually enough. Circumstances alter cases, however. When one's husband has to put up a log mill, one rises to the emergency, even though it means that there are a dozen or more men under foot.

A long arduous job faced Mr. Shaver and his crew that November of 1852. They had to convert standing trees into a buzzing sawmill by spring. With the faithful axe, trees had to be felled, trimmed, skinned, and chopped into logs of the required lengths. The logs had to be mortised and fitted into place. There were no nails, no planes, and no hardware for the finishing touches. Pegs, latches, everything had to be made out of wood by the skillful use of the axe.

This work took men, men took food, and Mrs. Shaver took the job of supplying the food. In fact, she was the answer, that winter, to a hungry man's prayer. The thought of that plucky

*Grandfather of Clyde, Craig and Myron Shaver of Wayzata.

woman feeding those men into strength and good humor, week in and week out, raises one's admiration to the point of reverence.

Even the modern housewife in a kitchen bristling with mixers and gadgets and bulging with fresh fruits and vegetables, canned goods, cake mixes, and bisquick might weary of a dozen men appearing three times a day for refueling.

Not so Sarah Shaver! She kept going, swishing her hoops and long skirts around her bare little cabin at an alarming speed. Fish had to be cleaned; wild ducks or geese needed picking and singeing; bread had to be set every day. And praise be, Jim had brought a sack of potatoes from St. Paul! How the men would snap up baked potatoes!

As yet, there wasn't another white woman around. Although she never saw one from November till the middle of January, Mrs. Shaver always had plenty of company. Her guests slipped in without rapping, without a sound from their moccasined feet. These Sioux women had their own wigwams all along the lake shore, but they liked Mrs. Shaver's little cabin much better. If they had stayed put, it would have been easier to manage the cooking, but they crowded around the white squaw, examining and tasting and using fingers for spoons.

One day Mrs. Shaver failed to call the men to dinner at the usual time. Her husband hurried home in alarm, threw open the cabin door, and found his wife in tears.

"Sarah, what's the matter?"

"Matter enough," she sobbed. "Look at those empty pie tins!"

"They're empty all right. What was in 'em?"

"Pumpkin pie till half an hour ago. Doesn't that make your ribs rattle? Oh, Jim," and her voice softened, "don't feel bad, you aren't to blame. It's just those tormented squaws."

"Squaws again! Why didn't you shoo 'em out?"

"I couldn't get rid of 'em. All five just hung around until those pies were out of the oven and cooling off. I stood right over 'em with the broom, ready to whack the first squaw that made a move, but they were too fast for me. Like a flash each one grabbed a pie and scuttled out, with me a-chasin' 'em, yellin' bloody murder."

Jim laughed in spite of himself. "Queer I didn't hear you."

"Oh, Jim, what wouldn't I give for the chance to pull every greasy hair out of their nasty heads!" Sarah continued her tale of woe, "I had put the dried pumpkin mother sent me into those pies—a surprise for you men. Honestly, I'm too mad to talk!"

"You're doin' mighty well at it." Jim grinned at his wife, but his tone was sympathetic.

Sarah Shaver had one more thing to say: "Jim, what does 'chichado' mean in Sioux?"

"Spoiled. Why?"

"Oh, that's the reason they scooped out the inside and just ate the crust. I feel like poisoning the whole gang." James burst out laughing, and so did Sarah. The storm was over.

For days after the pie episode, every Sioux stayed out of sight. Mrs. Shaver was elated at her sudden privacy. To her, this seemed to be the right moment to bring out the piece of pork she had been hoarding. It lay frozen and safely hidden under the trap door. Wild fowl and fish were not needed today; this time she really could surprise the men.

As the precious pork blubbered and boiled in the pot, it sent out a maddeningly delicious odor. She drew in long whiffs of that fragrance—and so did four braves who had followed the scent to its source. They had stolen into the kitchen while her back was turned and stood eyeing her and the boiling pot.

Taking a fork, the biggest brave solemnly approached the fire. He attempted to lift out the piece of pork, his eyes glittering with anticipation. In his haste, he made a false move and the meat fell back into its bubbling juice. Again he strove to get command of the situation.

This was the time for Mrs. Shaver to swing into action. Quickly she seized the teakettle full of boiling water and aimed its unerring stream straight at the busy brave's hands. With a splash, the pork fell back into the pot and went on boiling. Not a sound came from the amazed brave who stood motionless, gazing down at his hands. The other three grunted their satisfaction, crowded around Mrs. Shaver, patted her on the shoulder, and muttered "Tonka squaw, big squaw."

Minnetonka Story

"Tonka squaw" could do more than hold her own with the redskins and do the cooking for her crew. Aside from all this, in her first year of pioneering, she became Lake Minnetonka's first white mother, generously presenting this region with two little Shavers, Bernard and Bayard. And so it came to pass, in the summer of '53, that Minnetonka's twin babies began thriving and Minnetonka's sawmill started sawing.

WAYZATA

Only a Sioux could give full significance to the word "Wayzata." One of the earliest pioneers gave this explanation to a writer for the *Northwest Tourist*: "When a Sioux Indian gently croons out that word 'Wayzata,' you hear soft, balmy breezes sighing through the pines; but when he grunts out that same name with hissing vehemence, you feel the frosty, frigid breath of the north god whistling across the bay."

No other settlement around the lake has a more symbolic name. In seven letters, "Wayzata" wraps up "pines" and "north god" in such a neat parcel as to arouse every newcomer's curiosity. Is it true that pine trees once bordered Wayzata Bay? Did the north god ever sit among them in winter?

However that may be, somebody really did sit on the shore of that lovely bay in the summer of 1853, right where his Sioux ancestors had sat for ages past—Chief Shakopee and his braves.

Shakopee is the Sioux for six. Would you like to learn to count up to ten in Sioux? No trick at all—just remember to give the *ah* sound to the a's. In Sioux, the numerals are as follows:

1.	Onecha	6.	Shakopee
2.	No-pa	7.	Shako
3.	Yam-any	8.	Shakando
4.	To-pa	9.	Nep-chunk
5.	Zota	10.	Wix-chim-iney

Chief Shakopee was affectionately called Chief Little Six by the whites. He was of short stature for an Indian, built sturdy as an oak and graceful as a willow. He was manly, temperate, dignified, clean, and intelligent.

Among the wigwams encircling the shores of Wayzata Bay, almost in the great chief's lap, the little settlement of Wayzata was born when O. E. Garrison and A. B. Robinson staked out their claims. Chief Little Six was too broad-minded to fret about being crowded. People with great objectives in life are not the fussy sort, and Chief Little Six lived for just one great purpose—to save his people from drink.

After his own handsome son came to ruin through fire water, this grief-stricken Indian chief became a militant temperance reformer. Whenever he saw a bottle any where, at any time, full of any thing, he smashed it, just in case. Long, earnestly, and often, he pled with his people to have none of the white man's fire water, none of the Evil Spirit's poison.

While Chief Shakopee labored to keep his people sober, Gideon Pond, a missionary, was trying to reform the Indians around St. Paul and St. Anthony. In the *Dakota Friend*, published during the 50's, Mr. Pond wrote:

"Some years ago, the Indians bade fair soon to die together in one drunken jumble. They must be drunk. They could hardly live if they were not drunk. They would give all they possessed for whisky. It was made to drink, they drank it. Then they bit off each other's noses, broke each other's ribs and heads, and knifed each other. They killed each other with guns, hatchets, clubs, firebrands, fell into the fire and burned up, fell into the water and drowned. It is pleasant to record that after years of such fatalities, the best men of the Indian tribes everywhere became alarmed and united in a reform which was seconded by the missionaries, military officers, Indian agents, H. H. Sibley, and all respectable traders.

"Chief Little Six, I am told, is a great advocate of temperance out among the Minnetonka Sioux. Not much is known here of his work except that the Minnetonka Indians, coming into the trading posts, invariably stay sober, and quietly clear out when their business is done. Wish there were more like this great chief!"

Thus Chief Little Six was honored and respected by a white brother who had never seen him. Upon the very ground dedi-cated to temperance and to sober living by the beloved leader of his own race, the white settlement of Wayzata was established in 1853.

MOUND

Mound had a comparatively late start in life. The land around the rest of the lake had been preempted earlier. In 1876, the little village took shape among several groups of Indian mounds along the lake shore.

An early settler, Paul Hessing, wrote his neighbor back East about his experiences in the Mound vicinity in '55:

"In June, 1855, I went out from St. Anthony to what was then known as the 'Big Woods,' in the western part of Hennepin County. Went along the upper arm of Lake Minnetonka but ran into too many round knolls to suit me, so struck into the woods away back from shore.

"No roads, not even Indian trails, nothing but trees, vines, underbrush so thick the sun couldn't shine through. Tough work to cut your way through such interference! There was no evidence that anybody had ever been there. Too tired to keep on, I camped right in the woods, building me a fire to roast a partridge I'd shot. I lay down to sleep, but a headache kept me from sound slumber.

"It was about ten o'clock when I was startled by the sound of something stepping stealthily toward the spot where I was lying. I jumped up, and a big buck deer leaped several feet into the air with a snort which could have been heard a mile. Scared as I was, he must have been more so.

"In these woods I built a cabin in January, and my wife and I moved into it and lived there till spring. Then I built a better one covered with 'shakes' instead of poles and hay. 'Shakes' don't leak so much. Oh, the maple sugar and syrup we made that spring from the trees around the cabin! It makes my mouth water to think of it now. Imagine what a luxury this was for us when we hadn't any money to buy sugar — or anything else.

"One day I had to make a long trip to the next neighbor, and my wife had to stay alone. She said I had hardly got out of sight before she heard a little noise near the cabin. She looked out and beheld a company of twenty-four Indians. They turned out to be a band of Sioux on their way to fight the Chippewas around Shakopee. These tribes were the deadliest of enemies.

" 'Whisky-whisky-toback-toback,' is what they asked for as they entered the cabin. Nothing escaped their beady eyes. They made a raid on the cupboard, finding our precious maple sugar and drinking the maple syrup in noisy gulps. Not a crumb of anything was left.

"My wife was so thankful they didn't offer to molest her that she made no complaint about their cleaning up everything in the eating line. As they left the place, they gave an ear-splitting, blood-curdling war whoop which my wife always insists meant 'Thank you!' "

Five Little Towns and How They Grew

ST. ALBANS

St. Albans Bay—silent, secluded, and sunny, save for the shadows of leaning trees—still gives one the eerie feel of fays and fairies. One imagines water sprites balancing on swaying lily pads and wood nymphs back among the ferns, napping in nodding lady's-slippers. Undisturbed, St. Albans Bay was one of Nature's perfect poems.

This ethereal realm fell victim to a white invader several years after Excelsior had received its quota of pioneers. In 1856, Charles Morris found this cove and called it his Garden of Eden. Straightway he sent for Eve, his English bride.

Mrs. Morris, who had known wealth, affluence, and ease in her father's home, packed up her maids as a matter of course and brought them along. Some of us who had heard about this incident were delighted when that bride's daughter "Tiny" became reminiscent over the tea cups eighty years later.

We asked Tiny how her mother happened to bring her maids. "Well," she said, "Mother had never had to do one thing for herself. She couldn't imagine life without maids at her elbow. But nothing here looked good to those girls. They insisted on getting back to England as fast as possible.

"When Father took them to St. Paul to get the river boat, the bottom dropped out of Mother's world. She fairly fell into her 'going' chair and began rocking and sobbing. The faster she rocked, the harder she wept. On the point of hysterics, she suddenly thought of her Prayer Book. That might help. But could she find it? No! one of the maids had taken it by mistake.

"They say the English are plucky. That was Mother—she wasn't any hand to give up. No Prayer Book—so she knelt down by the 'going' chair and started in on the Lord's Prayer. She got as far as 'Give us this day our daily bread.' At that moment she opened her eyes. Over in a corner of the kitchen was the flour barrel looking straight at her, whispering 'daily bread, daily bread, daily bread.'

"Mother used to laugh and say that it took a flour barrel to change her outlook on life. At any rate, it gave her a great idea.

Wiping away her tears, she ran over to the neighbor's to find out how to make bread.

"That was the beginning of Mother's cooking campaign. It continued, in spite of a kitchen full of Sioux braves watching every move she made. They ate her first bread with relish—bless 'em—and drank her muddy coffee with gusto. She was good to them, and they rewarded her with their loveliest bead work and basketry.

"Did she learn to cook? Well, Father claimed she got to be the best cook around Minnetonka."

While Mrs. Morris was learning to cook, Mr. Morris was building a mill on the southeast shore of the bay. Soon other newcomers built their cabins nearby. Mr. Morris christened his new settlement St. Albans. A tiny hotel, a little Episcopal chapel, and the mill completed the miniature village. Not much of a settlement, but enough to turn this bay's pleasant poetry into pioneer prose.

EXCELSIOR

That same November, of 1852, while James Shaver was building the sawmill that became the embryo of Minnetonka Mills, George Bertram sat in his land office, 268 Grand Street, New York City, building his dream village on paper. In imagination, he saw himself back on the southeast shore of Lake Minnetonka, staking out the site for his proposed settlement.

What a day that had been for him last summer in the silence and solitude of unspoiled Nature! With startling vividness he recalled the full beauty of the El Dorado he had chosen for his dream village: the low, wooded hills rolling back from the water's edge, finally losing themselves in rich prairie land; the great stretches of water in front, reaching out and away for miles; the giant trees locking arms overhead; the tangled bowers of undergrowth sheltering little wild things; the throngs of sociable birds eyeing him with gentle curiosity.

Wonderful setting! Here his dream city would take form and be certain to rise higher and higher in the scale of development.

"Excelsior," the young man cried excitedly. "That's it—onward, upward, higher. That's what it means in Latin. By Jove,

Longfellow's idea is good enough for me, good enough for my village!"

Under the spell of this idea, Mr. Bertram seized his pen and began to write furiously. For days he had tried to formulate some sort of statement which prospective land seekers could sign and regard afterward as a binding bargain. At last he felt the emergence of success, as he read aloud the result of his inspiration.

"The Excelsior Pioneer Association, November 12, 1852, Preamble: Whereas, we the undersigned having associated ourselves into a body to remove to Minnesota Territory next summer, and occupy some of the government lands now vacated by the late treaty with the Sioux Indians, and having been on a tour of the Western States last summer, have selected a site for a village and farming country, that for healthfulness of climate, fertility of soil, beauty of scenery and nearness to markets, cannot be surpassed by any other locality in the country: being within 12 or 15 miles of the two most important towns of the territory (St. Paul and St. Anthony) and having a front on a lake navigable for steam and other boats over forty miles: its waters as clear as crystal and abound in fish. The land around the lake is also surrounded with natural meadow. The country is gently rolling and interspersed with the most beautiful timber the eye would care to look upon, consisting of sugar maple, black walnut, butternut, white oak and red oak, and a number of others: also with wild fruit, grapes and berries of almost every kind. The whole country, in fact, possesses almost everything the heart of man could wish for."

The constitution that followed stated the terms of membership in the Excelsior Pioneer Association: the payment of an eight-dollar registration fee, and one dollar a week until the expedition should leave in the spring of '53. Upon arrival at the site laid out, each signer would draw lots for an acre plot within the village itself, and for one hundred and sixty acres outside, near the settlement.

With his project thus streamlined into preamble and constitution, Mr. Bertram confidently hung out his sign in the face of Mr. and Mrs. Public:

Go West! Join the Excelsior Pioneer Association
Inquire—268 Grand Street

Judging from the stream of prospective land seekers that began to pour into Mr. Bertram's office, it would seem that most of the city of New York was thinking of doing just what the new sign suggested. Out of this flood of prospects, Mr. Bertram felt certain of at least three hundred who could be counted on to join the expedition going west about the middle of the following June.

The end of the first week in June found George Bertram locking up his office earlier than usual. Final arrangements for departure had to be made. And he wanted to hurry home—he had a surprise for Julia! In high spirits he threaded his way through the deafening traffic. "Never mind," he told himself, "not many more days of this devilish din. How Julia will love to hear the loons out there on Lake Minnetonka!" Pleasant thoughts sped him to his own door.

"Julia," he called, bursting in like a tornado, "Julia, we've got three hundred and fifty up to date!"

His young wife smiled indulgently. "If we don't look out," she said, "we'll be taking a big chunk of New York with us."

George looked pleased. "But say, Julia, I forgot the best part of the whole thing—it's done, all done!"

"What's done?"

"Why, our house—a two-story log house with shingles on it. McGrath says he and Wiley are proud of their job. And, do you know, those two fellows have got our bed made!"

Julia was puzzled. "Our bed made? What do you mean?"

"Well, when a pioneer builds his cabin, he puts up his bed at the same time, so he can use the end and side of his house for two sides of his bed. Here's the way."

George began to pace off the distance. "From the corner of the cabin the builder measures five feet out along the end like this, then down six feet or so, parallel to the side of the house. Now this would be the point to set up a post. From the post he nails boards to the end and side of the cabin. This completes his bedstead. All he needs then is poles for slats. It's best to nail these slats in place. Then it's ready for the tick of grass or wild hay. By Jove, isn't that a bed fit for a king and his queen?"

Before Julia could answer, George was off again. "Say, where did I put McGrath's letter?" He slapped his pockets anxiously.

"Oh, here it is. Believe I'll read you the first part of it. Gives a good idea of the country. Want to hear it, dear?"

"Why, of course." Julia felt that nothing could eclipse what she had just heard about the bed that she was expected to occupy. Her husband began:

"Dear Bertram: Wiley, Surveyor Christmas, and I started out to your location the first of May. We had a compass, so went direct to a small lake not far from your site. Going was hard — nothing but a tangle of vines and undergrowth.

"Well, just as we came to this little lake, a blizzard set in without a mite of warning. It got beastly cold. Mr. Christmas turned back to St. Paul. Now Wiley and I call that lake 'Christmas Lake' after Surveyor Christmas.

"We stumbled on trying to find Stephen Hull's place. We knew it was right out here somewhere, but where? Well, we lost our way; when we looked for our compass, we'd lost that, too!

"The third day, nearly frozen and starved to death, we stumbled into Hull's cabin. Guess we must have gone 'round in circles all right. But it's no wonder Hull's shanty was hard to find — it's over by a narrow neck of water * connecting the two parts of this big lake. The snow was still falling by the ton, and the temperature had sunk out of sight. A few hours more would have finished us, sure enough.

"You may not like Minnesota's climate, but you sure will like all the folks out here. They'd give you the shirt off their backs. Coming out yesterday, I met a fellow living on a claim ** a couple of miles or so east of your location. Henry Lyman's his name. I happened to mention I didn't have any cloth for bullet patches.*** Quick's a wink he tore off his shirt tail and gave it to me. How's that?

"All this May has been cold and damp and disagreeable, but we've kept right at your house — had such big appetites we ran short of supplies. The Indians, confound them, beg considerable off us all the time. Say! the Sioux are thick as hops 'round here. They don't look like they're leaving. Yesterday an old brave declared: 'Me no go.' Guess that's the way most of 'em feel about it."

"Well, that's just about all," George concluded. "Guess I told you the rest." He folded the letter carefully and returned it to his inside pocket.

*Now known as "The Narrows."
**This claim, now called Alfalfadale, is still in possession of the Lyman family.
***Guns of those days had to be loaded with bullets wrapped in little pieces of cloth.

Julia sat motionless. The first part of that letter brought her a sensation of deadly desolation, but the conclusion froze the depths of her imagination.

"Why, Julie, what's the matter? Have you got the ague?"

"Oh, George," she sobbed miserably, "look at me. What sort of pioneer will I ever make? I'd be petrified at the very sight of an Indian."

"Why, those fellows are friendly enough."

Her husband sounded reassuring, but Julia had other grievances. "And George, what kind of a country is that anyway, to have a blizzard in May? Don't they have any spring at all in Minnesota? How can anybody think of going to such a place?"

The truth is that most of the New Yorkers who signed Mr. Bertram's constitution never got any farther west than wishful thinking. His "Excelsior Pioneer Association" shrank to small proportions, but some of it arrived in due time, headed by George and Julia Bertram. Their new home was waiting for them on the spot where the Fenton house now stands. When Robert Mc-Grath had time to put up a house for himself, he built such a sturdy structure that it forms the nucleus of the present Dr. Hugh Arey residence.

Five Little Towns and How They Grew

Part II – THE FIVE SETTLEMENTS GROW INTO TOWNS

MINNETONKA MILLS

"It cannot be otherwise but that Minnetonka Mills will become a city of real import in the near future," prophesied the St. Anthony *Express* in the late 50's. Not often is a town as favorably located as Minnetonka Mills. Situated upon a lake and upon a swift-flowing stream as well, it secured the twofold advantage of lake commerce and water power.

Lake Minnetonka's first sawmill turned the nearby forests into the flooring, siding, and roofing needed by the new settlers for their log cabins. It provided lumber for building Minneapolis sawmills and flour mills and for the first bridge across the "Father of Waters." This little Minnetonka mill, with only a hundred workmen, turned out an amazing amount of lumber.

In 1854, Mr. Atwood established a modest furniture factory which used the best-grained wood for tables, chairs, and bedroom furniture. Today Atwood chairs and bedsteads are still doing service in some of our oldest lake homes.

Not only did the Minnetonka Mills settlement have the first lake port, the first sawmill, and the first furniture factory on the lake, but it also became the first distributing center for the rest of the lake region. To this center, from St. Anthony and St. Paul came supplies which, with Minnetonka Mills lumber and furniture, were shipped by batteaux to all points along the shore.

Gradually settlers drifted in. The busy mill spoke volumes to these newcomers. It offered them more comfortable log cabins with board floors instead of dirt floors and board roofs instead of poles covered with hay. This mill formed a center for a group of people living and working together in an untamed wilderness. Not far from the mill, a tiny log store was put up by Paschal Spafford, who kept a few groceries in front and a post office in one corner.

Newcomers were given a royal welcome and soon felt at home. In this new type of existence each needed the other's friendship and sympathy; each enjoyed the other's homespun jokes; each was ready to offer everything he had to a neighbor in need.

One day in '56 a Mr. Waters arrived with his wife and family from Pennsylvania by river boat. The poor man had contracted cholera during the boat trip and was seriously ill. Within a week he died, leaving Minnetonka Mills stunned by its first tragedy.

Mr. Waters was young—pioneers usually are. Old age has never been eager to go pioneering; it has always preferred its rocking chair in the chimney corner. In the youthful optimism of the Mills pioneers there had never been room for the thought of death; consequently, no one had thought of needing a coffin. The sudden necessity for such a commodity brought the populace together to solve an awkward problem. A man by the name of Gray, A. N. Gray, broke the silence: "I'll try my hand at making a coffin. Never made one, but I can try."

Mr. Gray did try and succeeded admirably. Again the people assembled, this time to examine the new coffin. "Good work," they all agreed, all except one young woman whose eyes filled with tears. "It's nice—very nice, but it looks so bare and hard."

Suddenly she left the crowd and hurried back to her cabin. Brushing aside her tears, she drew a low trunk from under the bed, opened it, and buried her face for a moment in the soft folds of the lovely garment lying there—her wedding gown. Gently she laid the beautiful dress over her arm, picked up her scissors, and hurried back.

By that time everybody had gone except Mr. Gray. He seemed grieved that he couldn't have made his coffin more restful for the departed one, but his face brightened as he caught sight of the young woman with the dress over her arm. Together they lined the last resting place for the new friend who had arrived just in time to move on again—across the Great Divide.

The next need of the settlers was a cemetery. Someone knew of a sightly spot and told of "the trees that were in the field, that were in all the borders round about." This location was chosen, and it became Groveland Cemetery. When the day of Mr. Water's burial arrived, no one stayed behind even to watch the mill. It, too, did honor to the departed by remaining silent that day.

Not many days after its first funeral, Minnetonka Mills had to go a-fishing. All at once Minnetonka's fish had apparently decided to take a trip down its outlet. The mill pond was a seething mass of fins and tails clogging the mill wheel, which refused to budge. People from the surrounding country were asked to come with pitchforks and ox carts to relieve the situation. They lifted tons of fish out of the mill pond and the stream itself before the mill wheel could revolve freely again.

Minnetonka Mills was the first of all the shore settlements to enter politics and join the rest of the state in governmental matters. W. S. Chowen, sent in 1857-58 to the legislature, had the honor of representing this lake region at the end of the territorial legislature and at the beginning session of the state legislature.

In Minnesota history, the year 1858 is remembered as the year Minnesota became a state; in Minnetonka Mills history, it is remembered as the year of dire disaster. In 1858, the sawmill and the furniture factory burned to the ground. People began to pack up and leave. Minnetonka Mills became a deserted village with only the mill pond and the dam left to tell the story of a brief bright past.

WAYZATA

Long-legged Sarah stood in the cabin door all curiosity. Pa was showing some men the wheat field out front. Finally, bidding his vistors farewell, he hurried home.

"Who were they, Pa?" Sarah asked.

"Oh, some fellows from the Mills. They'd heard the best stand of wheat in the country was right over here at Wayzata. Our wheat, Sarah! They kept asking where I got my seed—not a weed in the whole field!"

Almost before Pa's last word, Sarah was on her way to look at the field herself. That wheat stood for about everything that had happened to her since Pa brought the family out West in '56—only last year to be sure, but when a girl is fifteen, a year makes a big difference.

37

Sarah knelt to count how many stalks of precious wheat had "stooled out" from a single grain. Every stalk showed a plump sturdy head. Only a year ago this spot was timber land. She and Ma had helped grub it. It took blisters and back aches to get out what Pa and the oxen had left.

Before snowfall, Pa had declared the field was in good shape. The next job was to pick weed seed out of the wheat Pa had brought along from Ohio. Night after night before the fireplace, she had helped Pa and Ma and the boys discard the chaff and weed seed left in the wheat at threshing time.

Night after night, George Newell had dropped in to help. Sarah loved to hear him and Pa talk, until she got so hopelessly sleepy that her long legs could hardly carry her up the ladder to her breezy attic bed.

She had wondered that winter if spring would ever come, but it came in March, so Pa thought. He put in his wheat—a little early, the neighbors said. Pa knew he was right. He was sure of it, until a howling blizzard sent him to the bottom of despair. Nothing could convince him but that his wheat was ruined.

When the snow melted—Sarah smiled at the memory of it— there stood the wheat thick as hair. Every day they watched it grow. So did George. One day in June, the young girl ran out to the field to enjoy the wheat alone. And there was George. Right by that beautiful wheat, George told her a strangely sweet story, new to her.

When she hurried home with the news, her provident mother unwrapped some cloth she'd brought from back East, with glass buttons and stays, for the wedding dress. When the lovely gown was done, Ma hung it on Sarah's bed-post for her to enjoy until her wedding day, the twentieth of July which would be her sixteenth birthday.

The day of the wedding arrived. It was a beautiful day, but Ma had a splitting headache—too much sewing, too many nights out helping neighbor women in their hour of trial. "Now don't you worry a mite, child. I'm staying in bed till afternoon. I'll be all right with a little rest, and everything is ready for the—"

Before Ma could finish, there was a loud sharp rap on the

door. A neighbor from back in the woods stood there, pale with anxiety. Could Ma come quick? It was their first, so no telling what might happen!

"Sarah child," Ma spoke with great earnestness, "you'll have to go in my place. I'm no good with a sick headache. Now listen to every word I tell you, and you can manage."

The next few hours were crammed so full that Sarah didn't have time even to look out the window. The matter at hand was of absorbing interest.

After bathing the baby and laying him beside his mother, she seized her sunbonnet and started for home, but her feet failed to carry her even over her neighbor's back step. Instead, they flew out from under her as though the step had been smeared with soft lard. The ground all around her seemed to be moving. "I must be dizzy," she said to herself.

Dazed, she sat there trying to collect her wits. What was the matter with the world anyway? The ground was moving, and clicking, and snapping besides. Grasshoppers! Grasshoppers swarming up tree trunks, clinging to twigs, even hanging over the edge of her sunbonnet staring at her with beady black eyes. They were everlastingly chewing. What could they be eating? A glance at the leafless trees and bushes gave her the answer.

Horrified she got up and started to run for home. The footpath seethed and wriggled and hopped up to meet her. It was hard even to keep her balance. The strange clicking hum made by these little fiends filled the woods with weird foreboding.

As she neared home, she heard voices. Pa and the boys were running back and forth with torches, yelling like mad, stamping, jumping up and down, trying to turn the waves of grasshoppers aside from the precious wheat.

It would have been easier to turn back the ocean's incoming tide. In spite of all their torches and all the din, the grasshoppers were wholly unconcerned. They perched jauntily on big heads of wheat or trapezed from stalk to stalk, incessantly chewing.

Sarah hurried by—the sight was more than she could endure. The cornfield was bare. The long rows of peas were gone. Ma had planned on a mess for supper tonight. Poor Ma, how would her head be feeling by this time?

Just as Sarah came within sight of the cabin, the door was flung open. One of her little brothers was wielding the broom, heaving and pushing. It takes strength to sweep out buckets of grasshoppers. Suddenly a hideous fear gripped the girl's heart, her wedding dress!

With only "Are you better, Ma?" Sarah scaled the attic ladder two rungs at a time. A smothered cry of anguish escaped her as she took in the whole situation. The bed-post was bare, only a few stays and a sorry little pile of glass buttons remained to tell the story.

"Sarah," it was her mother's voice from the foot of the ladder, "don't cry, dear, just give me every stitch you've got on. I'll wash and iron what you're wearing. There's no time to lose. You can't disappoint George and all the neighbors. In a few hours George will be rowing Preacher Galpin over from Excelsior. Come, child, you can have a nice wedding anyway."

If the neighbors thought it was foolish to get married on the night of the grasshopper invasion, they did not say so. Everybody faced a dark future, but something might turn up—and it did.

In '57, China ran short of the very thing that grew in the Big Woods by the ton—ginseng. From the sweetish-tasting root the Chinese made a precious, life-giving drug. Ginseng they had to have. Through government agents they offered from four to eighteen dollars a pound for dried roots.

Sarah and George joined the neighbors in the hunt for roots. Soon Pa, Ma, and the boys joined the ginseng crusade. With George and Sarah to tell stories and sing a song now and then, this family developed into a champion crew. They learned that the trick to ginseng-ing is to conserve energy by using as few motions as possible. They brought up the root with a single stroke of hoe or hook, shook off loose dirt, and threw the root into pillow case or sack carried on their backs.

Freshly dug roots were incredibly heavy, but they became lighter as they dried out. Wayzata, the ginseng center for the

Minnetonka region, received boat loads of roots from Excelsior, St. Albans, and Mound. After thorough drying on Wayzata racks and a final inspection, they were taken by ox cart to St. Paul for shipment by river boat.

By the time the lake settlers had combed the Big Woods back to the prairie line in search of ginseng, the Civil War broke out. The ginseng era, from '57 to '61, was at an end. A definite change came over all the lake towns. Settlers began to leave for their old homes back East. When George Newell enlisted, Sarah, Pa, Ma, and the boys returned to Ohio.

* * *

During the Civil War there was no post office at all in Wayzata. That was too bad, because a certain Mrs. Day, the postmaster's wife, had thoroughly enjoyed her husband's position. From the time Wayzata's postal service was first established in '55, Mrs. Day had relieved her husband of any responsibility regarding personal mail—her petticoat pocket was just the place to keep letters safe and sound, near enough to examine in spare moments.

At the close of the Civil War, "Wayzata" dropped out of existence. This settlement was listed as Freeport in the United States postal guide. For the older settlers, however, the name "Wayzata" had vital significance; it commemorated the legends and lore of the Sioux who had vanished at the beginning of the Indian outbreak of '62. In a year's time the name "Wayzata" was reinstated for good.

MOUND

After looking through the names of Minnesota's pioneer towns, one returns to Minnetonka's tiny roster with relief. Every one of her little shore settlements bears a significant name. The name "Excelsior" is poetic; "Minnetonka Mills," practical; "Wayzata," legendary; and "Mound," realistic. Later lake settlements bear names that have at least a regional significance; "Ferndale," "Crystal Bay," "Deephaven," "Spring Park," and "Cottagewood" are examples.

The name "Mound" tells in five letters the story of a vanished race that has left its burial mounds as mute evidence of a past existence. No one in Mound needs to gossip about the neighbors nor talk about the weather, because there is before the people always just one vital question: Are these mounds the work of a prehistoric race of mound-builders, a race that was long ago pushed south into Mexico by the Indians, or are they of Indian origin?

Perched on the top of some twenty mounds itself, this town has become mound-conscious, though it has no monopoly on them. "Almost every bay and promontory has at least one or more mounds," say archeologists Brower and Winchell, who report 495 of them around Lake Minnetonka.

John Carver, early explorer and friend of the Sioux Indians, often watched these red men build their burial mounds in sightly spots along the banks of the Mississippi. "This method of burial," according to John Carver, "was certainly in use in recent times among our own Indian tribes. The custom of this imaginative people was to place the bodies of their dead upon stagings over-looking lakes, rivers, or exceptionally beautiful scenery which they would have enjoyed while living, and leave them there until at certain intervals they collected the remains for burial in the mounds. Investigations have revealed little except bones, and the evidence of great antiquity is not very clear."

It is of interest to note that archeologist Winchell believed that the mounds around Lake Minnetonka are of Indian origin.

As early as 1857, scientists and curious visitors from the East began to show interest in the mounds, especially those in the vicinity of Mound and Halstead's Bay. Sixty-nine mounds could be clearly seen on the shores of this little bay. After a visit to these mounds, Mrs. Harriet Bishop philosophized as follows: "By these mounds is the place to pause and think back centuries, to the times when the red men, children of the forest and prairie, hunted and fished; loved and hated; fought, rejoiced, sorrowed—and died—leaving scarce a mark behind them, save these mounds."

Mound City established its suburbs first, its circumference as it were. Then in the 70's the settlement began to fill in, taking on the shape of a real village. This is the way it came about.

Five Little Towns and How They Grew

Matthias Cook in '54 built a story-and-a-half hotel, 14 x 20, and established "Cook's Landing," thereby offering a humble welcome to any who might wish to visit that part of the Upper Lake. Mound opened its first school in 1860. Then came a blacksmith shop and later a grist mill. All were some distance apart.

Next the Carman boys, industrious young men, established a steam freight line between Wayzata and the few buildings standing aloof from each other along Cook's Bay. Somehow, the freight line gradually had the effect of centralizing the settlement, and when it secured a post office in '76, Mound City became a reality. Today, however, we are quite content to call this Upper-Lake town simply Mound.

ST. ALBANS

St. Albans never grew. That little town was "of few days and full of trouble." In this settlement's brief existence there was only one bright spot, a piece of red calico. An ardent parishioner, longing for a stained glass window in the little Episcopal log chapel, stretched a bit of scarlet cloth over the window above the altar. The effect was gratifying and this earnest worshipper felt highly elated—until his wife missed her best red petticoat.

As soon as the mill was built, it began doing a fair business. Its droning sound was sweet music in the ears of St. Albans, until one day its humming was completely swallowed up in the buzzing of myriads of wings. The grasshoppers had come!

Those grasshoppers left the country bleak and barren. However, there was one thing they did not eat—the roots of the ginseng plants—so St. Albans resorted to ginseng-ing with the rest of the pioneers around Lake Minnetonka.

When their little mill began running again, only small returns were realized. Finally, no money at all came in for mill work done. The financial panic of '57 had found even this tiny hamlet. There was no money, but the mill was still theirs. Then in '59, their mill burned to the ground.

"The sheltered cot, the busy mill
The decent church that topt the neighboring hill"

finally disappeared completely—St. Albans died.

Minnetonka Story

After a long absence, Charles Morris, the father of St. Albans, returned to Minnetonka. In the early 80's, he bought a thousand acres of land reaching from St. Albans Bay to Christmas Lake where he built his beautiful English country house, Glen Morris (later Radisson Inn).

EXCELSIOR

Within a few years after his arrival, George Bertram left the settlement he had established and moved his family to Monticello, Minnesota. The story of Excelsior's later development runs through much that follows, indicating that it came to occupy an important place among Minnetonka's towns.

| CHAPTER VI | *Minnetonka's* |
| | *Miracle Man* |

ONE of our carpenters had made us acquainted at lunch time
with the old Sioux squaw, Manitoucha. Now we were going to
be introduced by another workman to Excelsior's first minister,
the Rev. Charles Galpin.

"Sure, I knew 'im. I can prove it." Our friend pulled out an old
yellowed envelope. Down in one corner of it rested a small tooth.
"See there! Preacher Galpin pulled that tooth for me. It'll take a
couple o' lunch periods to tell you about 'im. Are you sure you
want me to?"

We were sure, so the speaker of the day cleared his throat and
began: "Of course bein' a preacher was his real trade, but of
all the things he could do besides! He had a head on his shoulders;
an' was he a go-getter? Why, he got here to Excelsior a good bit
ahead o' the rest o' that New York gang.

"Bein' a preacher, he come a-wearin' a tall silk hat, gloves,
and patent leather shoes—what there was left of 'em after walk-
in' over from Chaska, right through the woods. Very next
mornin' he begun swingin' the axe, gettin' logs ready for the
cabins the New York folks were gonna need. Pa allus said that
that preacher could turn a tree into a respectable log the fastest
of anybody he'd ever seen.

"Soon's Preacher Galpin and a couple o' carpenters got the
newcomers into their cabins, he begun organizin' 'em into a
church—an' could he preach! My folks 'lowed as how he could
put up the rippin'est sermon they ever hoped to hear. Funny
though, he allus acted sort o' relieved-like when the Sabbath was
over. Fact is, he said once that he liked Christianity best in everyday clothes.

45

Minnetonka Story

"Soon's he got the Excelsior church a-goin', he looked 'round for more prospects—found 'em, too, over in Chanhassen. A bunch o' Massachusetts colonists had settled there, an' say, they jumped at the chance to go in with the Excelsior folks. That's how the First Independent Church of Excelsior and Chanhassen come to be organized July 17, 1853. Yup, that was the day exactly. Pa and Ma heard that first sermon. His text was 'Now then we are ambassadors for Christ.' He figured that was a big enough job for us human bein's.

"The settlements took turns back an' forth at havin' church. When Chanhassen come over to Excelsior, they had services under the trees north o' where Trinity Chapel is now—under the biggest trees you ever saw.

"After he got the church goin' he took a look at the little log schoolhouse. 'Excelsior can do better,' he told the school meetin' he'd called. Fact is, he had a whole school system up his sleeve an' he wanted a bigger place to put it. When Preacher Galpin got through explainin' his ideas, the people voted unanimous to start a two-story schoolhouse out o' logs the next mornin'. An' they did—right where the grade buildin' is now.

"Where to get teachers was the next question. Preacher Galpin volunteered his services to help out. An' could he teach? Bless you, the kids told such tall stories about their good times at school that the young folks asked for 'im to teach night school. Ma and Pa went one winter, before they had us young-uns underfoot.

"Preacher Galpin sure liked people, 'specially young-uns. While he'd be talkin' to my folks, he'd allus keep rubbin' my head —felt powerful good someway. One day I was fishin' in a first-class little river that used to run behind the store buildin's on the west side o' main street, 'twas quite a stream from springs back up 'round Murray Hill an' good fishin' too. Well, one day I was havin' luck when whir-r-r, a fishline whizzed past my left ear— an' there was Preacher Galpin! Then he come an' set down by me.

"It was easy talkin' to 'im; you jus' told him everythin' before you knew it. We talked an' talked. Blamed queer he'd take so much pains with a barefoot young-un like me, but he acted 's if I

46

was doin' 'im a big favor to let 'im set down by me an' rest. Said he never had much time to fish, folks were usually comin' after 'im if somebody got turrible sick or broke his leg, or if somebody wanted to get married or have a funeral or get a tooth pulled or have their land surveyed—well, there jus' wasn't much time to go fishin'.

"He told me how he'd paid his way through college workin' for a dentist an' a doctor. On the way home from fishin' he took me to see his tool room. He had a whole kit o' dentist tools, but his surveyin' outfit was somethin' to look at. Said he'd learned surveyin' from his father 'fore he left home to work in his uncle's tin shop.

"Pa said Preacher Galpin could survey anythin'; fact is, the village of Excelsior still runs 'long his plattin' lines. Yes, sir! that man could turn his hand to anythin'. Never heard the beat o' the things he could do.

"One day Pa an' the boys tapped fifty trees too many for the sap pails we had, so while they were wonderin' what to do, Ma called me in . . . she was excited. 'Run to Excelsior quick, find Preacher Galpin an' ask him to make us fifty sap pails. Be quick, an' say *please*, mind you.'

"How well I remember that March mornin': sun a-shinin' through the bare branches overhead makin' queer shadows on the meltin' snow, little streams o' water tricklin' 'long, a lazy feelin' in the air—'fifty sap pails, fifty sap pails!' I started runnin' faster, sayin' it over an' over for fear I'd forget. The grouse were a-drummin', the woodpeckers a-tappin'—'fifty sap pails, fifty sap pails.' What if Preacher Galpin should be gone, what would a fella do then? 'Fifty sap pails, fifty sap—' There he was, stridin' 'long towards the lake. I tried to get up 'nough more steam to catch 'im. No use, so I jus' took in a big breath an' hollered with all my might, 'Fifty sap pails, fifty—.'

"Preacher Galpin heard me. He turned 'round, an' did he laugh? I couldn't say a word—not 'nough breath left for even 'fifty sap pails.' After a minute or so, I told him how Ma was worryin' 'bout the sap goin' to waste. He laughed again, pleased-like—that's the way he allus acted when somebody needed help

47

—real pleased-like. 'They'll be ready tonight at seven,' he said, 'so come get 'em then, an' put 'em up for the early run tomorrow mornin'.'

"That was jus' like Preacher Galpin to figger it all through fast. Don't ask me how he made them sap pails—he jus' did, that's all.

"Never saw the Preacher try his hand at drivin' oxen, presume he could though. Any rate, he could drive that fractious match team o' sorrel Morgans o' his. They'd run at the drop o' the hat for anybody else, but not for the Preacher. No, siree! They acted like ole plugs the minute he come 'round. That was his mail team. With that team he hitched this lake up to the rest o' the world by bringin' the mail back an' forth, to an' from St. Anthony an' St. Paul. He brought more'n mail—he brought buttons an' thread an' nails an' rivets an' whalebone stays for dresses, an' passengers besides.

"Bet you're a-wonderin' how the Preacher come by a team o' horses when everybody else was drivin' oxen. Well, sir, he come by 'em honest, but sharp-like. 'Twas this way. The church wanted a change—lan' knows why. Guess the church folks wanted a minister that'd give all his time to religion. Leastways, they called a new preacher. Sheldon, Rev. Charles Sheldon, was his name. He started from Ohio with horses an' carriage, an' his family, o' course. Long ways, nigh a thousand miles, an' no roads to speak of. Besides, had to stop on the way to have a baby. Well, sir, guess he thought he'd find more'n thirty-six folks in Excelsior. All o' them was safe in the fold already—even the babies baptized. Preacher Galpin had been purty thorough.

"The church felt good over havin' a new preacher, but they'd never thought o' how to pay 'im or where to put 'im. Preacher Galpin had allus taken care o' himself an' his wife—but Preacher Sheldon had four young-uns already. What was to be done? It was a tight place for the church folks, but Preacher Galpin come to the rescue. Said he'd a notion to go out to his log house, out in the country a ways, an' so he'd sell his house to Preacher Sheldon in payment for the minister's horses and carriage, the sum o'

forty dollars, an' the minister's promise to preach for nothin'
until the congregation could agree on his salary.

"I want to tell you right here that it woulda been mighty easy
for them two preachers to be at loggerheads. But say, it wasn't
long 'fore folks called 'em David an' Jonathan. They got to be
the best friends you ever saw, an' they didn't act exclusive either
when an Episcopal preacher by the name o' Chamberlain put up
the little Trinity Chapel and held services there. Preacher Galpin
and Preacher Sheldon received 'im with open arms, you might
say. Reverend Sheldon kept the Excelsior church goin' while
Preacher Galpin went to all sorts of out-o'-the-way places bringin' the Gospel to folks who hadn't heard a sermon since comin'
West.

"Well, the last great big thing Preacher Galpin did, 'side from
preachin' powerful good sermons every Sunday, was to build a
steamboat. The day come when the *Governor Ramsey*, as he
called his boat, was ready to put out to sea. Folks come for miles
'round. All the hills and shores was crowded. People cheered
an' cheered. Everybody was wild with enthusiasm. All of us
little tads was down at the water's edge, crowdin' right up as
near's we could. 'Skipper' Galpin stood on deck, wavin' at the
people and bowin' when they cheered.

"Suddenly he hurried down from deck, ran across the gang-
plank straight toward us young-uns. 'Come on,' he said, 'you're
goin' t' help me take the first mail over to Minnetonka Mills.'

"Well, I dunno to this day how I ever got across that gang-
plank, but I did, an' so did the rest o' the fellas. We waved to the
folks on shore 's we stood on deck with 'Skipper' Galpin. I felt
dizzy-like with pride. Yes, sir! that was the biggest moment of
all my life, I can swear to that.

"An' that wasn't all. When we got to Minnetonka Mills, we
had to put the mail bags right into the stage coach bound for
St. Anthony and St. Paul. The crowd had hung 'round on shore
to see us come back, an' that same dizzy feelin' got me again.
Nothin' serious—you always feel that way when pride puffs
you up to the breakin' point.

"Preacher Galpin was a great man with a great dream. For

years he'd hugged that dream to his heart—workin', savin', hopin', prayin', talkin', with one great aim, the realizin' o' that dream. Why, would you believe it, he'd got all the rest of us dreamin' his dream 'long with him. Even Ma'd say, every now an' then, 'Mind your manners, children, 'cause we'll be havin' a college here in town some day. That's somethin' to live for!' Preacher Galpin allus told us that the very first time he looked out over Lake Minnetonka, he felt that here was a perfect site for a college. One day he told Preacher Sheldon 'bout his dream. Almost before he'd finished, Preacher Sheldon grabbed him by the hand sayin', 'Let me dream 'long with you, brother.' So Excelsior had two dreamin' parsons, but they was too smart to keep dreamin' without some good reason. Fact is, the big guns o' the Congregational Church gave the matter favorable consideration; they even come an' looked Excelsior over, vowin' it was an ideal location.

"Preacher Galpin kept on hopin' an' prayin' that the Congregational Assembly would decide on Excelsior for their college. He set his mind onto that college with the most alarmin' determination, an' tried to make Excelsior a fit place for it. He even went to the Assembly himself to state the case. He was willin' to give all he had to make his dream come true.

"By this time the Preacher was makin' more money all the time with his dentistry an' was goin' reg'lar to Faribault an' Austin an' on south—dentists were purty scarce them days. Money was comin' in from his steamboat too. Purty soon he'd have money 'nough to bring his dream to life, he said.

"Just to try out his college scheme while the big men in the Congregational Assembly were discussin' Excelsior as a location for a new church college, Preacher Galpin hired a couple o' teachers from the East and set some college classes goin' on a small scale. Young people come from all 'round. The beginnin' was a big success.

"Then one day word come that the new college was to be built in Northfield on the banks o' the Cannon River, 'stead of in Excelsior on the shores of Minnetonka. Yes, sir! Excelsior'd lost out on gettin' Carleton College. 'Twasn't Preacher Galpin's fault, but his dream was gone. Jus' little College Lake, 'cross from Galpin Lake, is all we've got left o' that great dream.

" 'Poor Preacher Galpin,' everybody said, 'how'll he stand the blow?' No wonder they felt that way—the greatest dream o' his life had gone up in thin air. Well, for a week or so he looked dazed-like, pale an' absent-minded. He was tryin' to get the upperhand o' that cruel disappointment. At last, he jus' said, 'Thy will be done,' an' that's all there was to it—no complainin' nor blamin' of anybody. It was nothin' short of a miracle to see 'im come out of it the way he did.

"Well, sir, in a couple o' weeks he was himself again, as full of get an' go as ever. An' then he got a new idea. If Excelsior couldn't have a college, it could at least build a new Congregational Church—an' it did. He an' Clark, a friend o' his, donated the site. The two preachers helped put in the basement, begun it in 1870. The church itself was built an' dedicated the next year.

"Then one freezin' cold day, a fellow from across the lake somehow sunk his barge loaded with bolts. He was in a jam. Preacher Galpin'd know what to do, an' right off he come with a crew an' engineered the work so's they lifted the barge an' saved the bolts. That was good, but the exposure was more'n the Preacher could stand. Next day he died.

"Jus' sixty years old exactly—nice neat sixty years, from 1812 to 1872. Purty near all his las' twenty years he'd spent a-liftin' an' inspirin' an' a-tryin' to help us lake folks. He was an 'ambassador' sure 'nough. Remember? 'Now then we are ambassadors for Christ.' Guess that's why he was always workin' some little miracle or other for anybody that needed help."

CHAPTER VII | *Difficult Days*

MINNETONKA'S calendar for the years following the arrival of her white settlers is generously marked with difficult days—in heavy type. It was a sad day for Minnetonka's lordly trees and superabundance of game when she exchanged the red man's way of life for the white man's culture.

It was the day of doom for Minnetonka's Sioux when their Chief Little Six explained to them, in the summer of '52, that the Traverse Treaty would give their paradise to white settlers the following spring. Never before had they known uncertainty, but what was to become of them now?

Of one thing the Sioux were certain: wherever they might be, they would need food and clothing. Dried deer meat and deer skins could be prepared ahead of time. One day that summer Stephen Hull was staking out his claim near the Narrows when he caught sight of a hundred braves jogging along the nearby trail, each with the carcass of a freshly killed deer slung over his shoulder.

The redskins were bent on leaving nothing behind for the white invaders. They succeeded so well that, according to Robert McGrath's diary, all the meat the pioneers could scare up for their first Thanksgiving dinner in '53 was one raccoon.

Food was scarce, and hungry days were unpleasant. Men ranged the Big Woods for game with little success. Women and children scoured the region for wild strawberries, raspberries, gooseberries, and choke cherries. Housewives dried corn, pumpkin, and strawberries.

One woman who left a dozen quarts of strawberries spread on the kitchen table for a last drying had a surprise awaiting her when she returned a couple of hours later from a visit at the neighbors. She found a pair of squirrels desperately trying to escape from the kitchen through holes in the chinking. No use— the dried strawberries inside their insides were rapidly regaining their original size, while the holes in the chinking refused to stretch. A squirrel pie for supper was the solution.

Minnesota winters brought difficult days of extremely bitter cold for Minnetonka pioneers who had, for the most part, come from "white-collar" jobs in stores, shops, and offices. One old-timer used to say that he didn't get warm all that first winter in spite of wearing six shirts, three pairs of drawers, and six pairs of socks at one time. But pioneers did possess one enviable item of wearing apparel. Everybody had a tippet. Everybody wrapped his tippet round and round over head and ears and face and nose, leaving only a narrow slit for his eyes. It was a fine institution unless one's breath froze one's nose fast to one's tippet.

One day a Mound man came home after a cold day's work in the woods with his boots frozen to his feet and his whiskers frozen to his shirt. His boots resisted every bootjack in the house; his whiskers refused to be loosened. As a last resort, his wife suggested cutting off both boots and whiskers. No, he needed them! Finally, she rolled in the barrel used for scalding hogs and filled it with hot water—and her husband. That turned the trick. The ice king came off with both boots and whiskers intact.

People turn pioneers to better themselves and to make their dreams come true, yet early settlers around Minnetonka saw their dreams of future prosperity fade with each successive year. Farmers accustomed to manual labor would have cleared their land with fewer back aches and greater speed. Excelsior's founder, you recall, sat in his New York office and dreamed how his colonists could live in town and run their 160-acre farms on the outskirts. Mr. Bertram learned that long-handled farming was a difficult proposition.

Topping her other troubles, the grasshopper scourge followed by the financial panic of '57 left Minnetonka flat. Pioneers in this lake region seemed even worse off than those in prairie country where a settler could plow under a carpet of wild flowers in a jiffy and sow a field of wheat without delay. A Minnetonka pioneer had to wrest every inch of soil away from a greedy forest; moreover, returns were slow and slight in proportion to the labor expended.

Dark days were ahead, everybody agreed. Then came the dawn of the ginseng era when good hard cash began coming like manna in the desert.

At the close of an unusually profitable ginseng season, a dancing party was staged on plank platforms in the open. A level spot just out of Wayzata, they say, was chosen for this particular celebration, which was to last from Saturday night until Monday morning.

People came from every direction by boat and by ox team. The merrymakers bundled up their babies and parked them on piles of marsh hay; older children slept just anywhere; and the slow-moving oxen were turned loose to graze along the shore of the bay.

All Saturday night the dance went on by moonlight. Sunday morning the "pillars" of the church rowed across the lake to Excelsior for the services. The Rev. Charles Sheldon's sermon that morning sprang from the text "Blessed are they which do hunger and thirst after righteousness: for they shall be filled." A great promise, and it was a great sermon—but not great enough to pin down the wandering thoughts of some of his listeners. In spite of themselves, they kept longing for "the fleshpots of Egypt" across the lake.

Heroic souls! There they sat in person, but not in spirit. Upon their return, the dance was still in progress. The black sheep had kept the thing going. However, the tempo of the party quickened with the return of the "pillars," whose appetite for fun had been whetted to a keener edge by their hours of worship.

Church life and occasional dances took care of spiritual and social needs. Mental stimulus was furnished by the activities of a round-the-lake literary society. It gave one a definite lift to have debated as well as Henry Clay or to have rivaled Daniel Webster in oratory. It proved the balm of Gilead for back aches and blisters.

Later this literary society, becoming altruistic, suggested that the lake children should have better school buildings. It seemed like a minority's high-brow scheme; it meant money! The majority declared there was no money for such building schemes. Besides, Minnetonka Mills and even St. Albans had pretty fair log schoolhouses already, and Excelsior had a two-story school, the best around the lake. Then there was Mr. Gribble up at Mound giving his house to the young ones for a school. Ben Keesling in Wayzata had just asked Bill Pendergast to keep school in his cabin, so everybody was doing all right without new schoolhouses.

Suddenly controversial community matters were lost in the darker storm of national disaster; the Civil War was at hand. Minnetonka men hastened to answer the call. What would happen now with the men gone? How would the Indians behave toward a defenseless population?

The year, 1862, brought the answer. Word came that the Sioux were assembling at New Ulm. Chief Little Six and all his tribe left overnight. News of wholesale massacres perpetrated by the Sioux opened up a campaign of nerves among Minnetonka settlers.

Panic-stricken, many fled headlong for Fort Snelling. Ox carts were slow in such an emergency, but they were better than nothing. People loaded up their families and their valuables and gee-hawed their teams toward the Fort. Some brave souls stayed behind and built a stockade around the little Episcopal church, Trinity Chapel (at that time located opposite the present Excelsior Fire Department). Preacher Galpin kept his steamboat ready to take Excelsior-ites to Big Island in case of an Indian raid.

Nothing, absolutely nothing, happened anywhere around this lake. Why did the Sioux spare this region? Was it because their God Manitou, according to old Manitoucha, had loved this lake, and because his chosen red children had consecrated this region to peace? Had these Sioux obeyed their medicine men and refrained from bloodshed to escape the curse of the "rolling head"? Whatever the answer, no harm came to the whites of this region.

Adding to the gloom of those dark Civil War days, Lake Minnetonka began to sink with distressing rapidity. Islands and sand bars never seen before began to put in an unwelcome appearance. No figures as to the actual drop of the lake's water level are available, but it is reported that the people of Wayzata became thoroughly alarmed at the threatened loss of the lake. With the close of the War, however, the rain descended and the floods came, literally. Veritable cloudbursts brought the lake back to normal depth barely in time for the return of the soldiers.

The boys in blue came home to a full lake and to empty larders. There was little to eat but fish and game, and the season was too far advanced to put in a crop. Paper money was of little value, the government was "broke," hard times had come, business was dead. There was nothing to do but to stand around with one's teeth in one's mouth and one's hands in one's pockets. What next? The answer came from a wholly unexpected quarter.

One summer morning in 1866, Minnetonkans found their back yards buzzing with activity. "Massa an' Missie an' de chillun" were directing the unloading of pots and pans and Confederate tents by their colored folks.

"Massa" explained that the "war of the liberation" had put them into such a muddle they had had to come north to rest and think things through. A Fort Snelling officer had once mentioned Lake Minnetonka up in Minnesota, so—here they were.

Tired of camp cookery, these gay, spirited southerners made daily raids on Minnetonka's two little log hotels: George Galpin's at Excelsior and Matthias Cook's at Mound. They might, however, appear at some cabin door as paying guests. Minnetonkans found feeding them better business than raising wheat for grasshoppers.

Those southerners had come to rest. But who could rest alongside a lake teeming with fish and a woodland bulging with cherries and berries and game? Besides, who could miss mail days when Preacher Charles Galpin gathered up the lake's outgoing mail. His 50-foot sidewheeler, the *Governor Ramsey*, held an amazing number of passengers.

At Minnetonka Mills, a stagecoach from St. Paul waited to exchange its passengers, supplies, and incoming mail for the outgoing mail.

Those southerners vowed they would bring the rest of Dixie back with them the next summer. A railroad was coming too. The St. Paul and Pacific Company was planning to complete a track to Wayzata.

In the midsummer of 1867, train loads of southerners steamed into Wayzata to find the same little old *Governor Ramsey* puffing patiently. Thirteen years later those guests would have seen 90 handsome steamboats racing into port with clanging bells, ear-splitting whistles, and flame-belching smokestacks.

Galpin's and Cook's bulged. What about the overflow? Lake householders undertook to answer that question themselves. Each built a shelter for his family, leaving the house to the newcomers. Minnetonka's difficult days were rapidly slipping into days of excited anticipation.

| *Hotel Days*

Part 1 — THE FIRST HOTELS

Sᴏᴍᴇᴡʜᴇʀᴇ in "Brer Rabbit," Uncle Remus tells a little boy about a rabbit that climbed up into a tree. "But," objected the small listener, "rabbits don't climb." "Dis heah rabbit did," explained Uncle Remus, "he jes hed ter climb. De dawgs wuz aftah 'im."

From 1867 on, Minnetonka "jes hed ter climb"—the southerners were after her. When several thousand guests come knocking at the door, something has to be done about it.

Matthias Cook, the lake's pioneer hotel man at Cook's Landing, Upper Lake, was first to act. In all haste, he added to his old log hotel a three-story 56 x 42 addition affording accommodation for fifty guests. George Galpin, in Excelsior, followed suit by building an ample front onto the old Galpin House. From that time on this hotel was called the Excelsior House. It stood not far from the present Tonka Theater.

Other Minnetonka hotels gradually came into the picture, as the following list indicates:

Place	Name	Date	No. of Guests
Excelsior	Long View	'67	50
Upper Lake	Lake View	'69	50
Wayzata	Minnetonka House	'71	25
Wayzata	Gleason House *	'71	30
Excelsior	White House	'72	30
Excelsior	Appledore House	'74	30
Mound	Chapman House	'75	80 or 90

*The Gleason House still stands behind the Wayzata Community Drug Store and serves as a rooming house.

Hotel Days

Place	Name	Date	No. of Guests
St. Albans Bay	May House	'77	60
Minnetonka Mills	Newark House	'73	50
Excelsior	Slater House	'79	50
Mound	Bartlett House	'79	80
Shady Isle	Harrow House	'79	60

Every season more guests, like summer birds, were flocking to this northern lake of ours. More, many more hotels were needed. Gradually boarding houses began to piece out Minnetonka's hotel accommodations.

The Harrow Boarding House at Deephaven occupied one of the lake's choicest locations overlooking Carson's Bay. In '78, Sir Charles Gibson purchased this house to secure its site for his beautiful St. Louis Hotel.

There was an interesting boarding house in Linwood. When I asked Mrs. Nellie B. Wright how her father happened to build it there, she explained: "Well, the Minneapolis and St. Louis railroad started us. It was going across a corner of our place. The construction gang would be along in the spring, so Pa decided to build a big square house and get ready for 'em.

"Every morning that winter, long before daylight, Pa'd hitch up our little Indian pony to the sled and start to Minneapolis for lumber. Late every night on the way back, just before he'd get to Minnetonka Mills, a pack of wolves, howling fit to kill, would start following him. If anything went wrong with his lantern, he'd drag chains behind to scare 'em off.

"By early spring our new house was ready. It was plumb full of bedrooms with three tiers of bunks apiece fitted up with corn-husk ticks and comforters.

"There was a washbowl and pitcher on a little corner shelf in every room. Ma tacked a calico curtain along the edge of that shelf to hide the pail underneath, an all-right plumbing system for those days. Every room had its own lamp on a wall shelf.

" 'To sleep' a construction crew is easier than 'to eat' them, but it can be done. The bread those men could put away! Poor Ma had to bake every day all day long, but Pa helped her. He got a 30-gallon crock and then sharpened a two-by-four, planing

59

it nice and smooth. As soon as Ma had the flour and things in that crock, Pa went at it with his two-by-four. When Ma said it was mixed enough, Pa threw the dough onto the table and kneaded it with all his might. Then Ma put it into pans, three loaves at a lick.

"The gang came and went; and say, were we proud of the shining track they left behind them! Pa said that tourists would soon be poking all around our back yard, leastways he was sure we'd better get ready for 'em. You see we had some cash on hand from the construction gang, so out came the bunks to give Pa a chance to plaster. Then, in came beds and bureaus and looking glasses. My land, but that was exciting—all that new stuff!

"The plumbing and lighting systems stayed the same, but we made the other changes barely in the nick of time. That very night, before Ma could even get the beds made, several families of summer folks took possession of our quarters.

"You know," Mrs. Wright smiled at the memory of it, "Ma sure was an efficiency expert all right, the way she could get work out of the Swedish hired girl and little me. My first job every morning was to peel a bushel of potatoes; next came the dishes, then sweeping the kitchen and back steps. For a rest, I could hull a dishpan full of strawberries for the sheets of short-cake Ma already had in the oven.

"Whenever the men guests wanted to go fishing, Pa would row them around all day for $2—fine wages at that time! Like as not they'd bring home so many fish, Ma and Pa would be up all night cleaning 'em. Next day we'd have fish every meal.

"Sounds like work, but boy! we had fun too. In front of our Linwood House was, the finest sort of a beach. It was a secluded spot, so folks didn't need bathing suits. The women wore Mother Hubbards and the men used everyday pants, but the kids followed along in any sort of old thing. Swimming was done dog fashion, and nobody'd ever heard of diving. The same families came year after year, vowing they had more fun at our place than in some big hotel, and there were plenty of 'em being built around the lake, I can tell you that."

Boarding houses and hotels told only part of the story, as far as summer people were concerned. As the number of visitors increased, ordinary householders began bidding for patronage in earnest. Even farmers joined the ranks of advertisers, expressing themselves somewhat as W. H. LeVan chose to do in his "ad":

"All persons desiring a pleasant country boarding place in full sight of lake and big boats, with plenty of good substantial farm grub, come this way! Low rates. Good cooking! Plenty of chicken, ham, sausage, fruit, berries, vegetables. Come this way!"

Part II – THE BIG HOTELS

The year 1880 brought what this popular lakeside had been longing for—big hotels and big boats. Minnetonka, still wearing the earmarks of pioneer life, found herself a fashionable watering place.

If Samantha Allen, popular humorist of the 80's, had brought husband Josiah out from New York's Saratoga Springs to Minnesota's Saratoga, she would have found Minnetonka doing things in a big way. This naive couple might have fallen down Hotel Lafayette's elevator shaft, or become tangled in the long silky nap of that hotel's red velvet carpeting, or worse, they might have electrocuted themselves on Hotel St. Louis' five-mile system of electric bells.

Perhaps Samantha and Josiah would have met with no greater misfortune than getting lost somewhere on Minnetonka's miles of hotel verandas. However, that might have proved a piece of good luck. On those verandas they would have seen Minnetonka's guests at their best—laughing, talking, singing, taking no thought for the morrow, even entertaining Dan Cupid on the sly. On those porticos, that up-country couple would have seen men become chivalrous; ladies, coquettish; young folks, hilarious. Without doubt, the Allens would have returned to Saratoga Springs, recommending "more verandas, the bigger the better."

LAKE PARK HOTEL, later TONKA BAY HOTEL. "Veranda crazy" is what people called the architect of Minneonka's first great hotel, Lake Park, built across from Excelsior on Gideon's Bay. "Every room on a veranda" was the slogan.

Rain or shine, Lake Park's parlors were deserted in favor of her immense porches where guests, laying aside formality, enjoyed each other while getting the full value of the invigorating breeze off beautiful Gideon's Bay.

The day came when those verandas swayed with the gayest of gay crowds watching the rowing races charted from Excelsior to Lake Park. Years later this veranda-ed Tonka Bay Hotel became the great convention center of the Middle West. Verandas had proved their value.

HOTEL LAFAYETTE. When James J. Hill chose the highest point on the circumference of our lake for his Hotel Lafayette, people gasped. How had that prize location been overlooked so long? Jim Hill hadn't overlooked it. The truth is, he had kept that precise location in mind ever since all the horses in St. Paul had had the sleeping sickness in '72.

That winter there was not a team left to bring St. Paul-ites their winter's wood from the surrounding country. That was Jim Hill's opportunity. He hustled out to Minnetonka, bought standing timber, and set his lumberjacks to work—with orders to spare every tree growing on one particular spot. The firewood was shipped into St. Paul from Wayzata via the Great Northern.

In 1879, James J. Hill returned, a railroad magnate with well-lined pockets. He went straight to his cherished location. In the midst of the great trees he had spared with such care, he laid out the finest hotel west of New York City, Hotel Lafayette. (The Lafayette Club House now occupies that site.) From each of its eight hundred rooms there was a fine view of either the Upper or the Lower Lake.

Some have called the Lafayette a palace; others, a veritable Castle in Spain. Suffice it to say, it was the last word in equipment and splendor. Its grounds possessed all the natural grandeur of ancient trees that cast a thick shade over swaying hammocks, inviting all who passed to swing away their leisure hours.

HOTEL ST. LOUIS. Although a railroad king built Hotel Lafayette, an English knight headed the enterprise that established Hotel St. Louis at Deephaven. When Deephaven Park was a wild woodland with only a wagon road angling its shady way through trees and brush, people whispered about Sir Charles Gibson, its absentee owner. He was a short, keen-eyed, well-to-do man with a persuasive manner and a circle of wealthy friends in the city of St. Louis.

Sir Charles maneuvered his friends into a corporation that chose the Harrow House location, the present site of the Walter Douglas residence* as the spot for a new hotel, Hotel St. Louis. If the Lafayette was a thing of splendor, the St. Louis proved to be something that stood for American aristocracy—not eastern, but southern. Facing Carson's Bay and the Bay of St. Louis, the new hotel gave evidence of careful design and excellent architecture—Sir Charles abhorred the shoddy and the showy. Erected in '79, the Hotel St. Louis was ready within a year to entertain its exclusive clientele of four hundred guests.

The hotel furnishings were comfortable and elegant. Marble-topped dressers and tables, rich draperies, soft carpeting—everything was in correct taste for that time. When the hotel was wrecked in 1907, its furniture found its way into many of our lake homes.

Behind the hotel was a long row of neat white cabins for colored servants brought along to take care of the "chillun" of the southern aristocrats. Guests arrived by the Minneapolis and St. Louis, or by the spur run up to the hotel door by the Chicago Milwaukee.

It was at San Antonio, Texas, that a bit of good fortune came my way while waiting for a bus. The juke box had just played "By the Waters of Minnetonka," so I asked a nurse sitting next me if she knew that song.

"Know it? How could I help it when my patient tells me every day about his summer there in Hotel St. Louis? Minnetonka means heaven to Judge Weatherby."

At her invitation I called the next day, hoping her patient might feel strong enough to see me. The nurse said he was waiting for me. He lost no time in preliminaries—how long had Hotel St. Louis kept going after he was there in '80? How near did I live to the spot where it used to be? Satisfied with my answers,

*Now the home of B. C. Gamble.

63

he lapsed into the past. He began by telling how cool it was on those long verandas looking off toward the lake.

"You see," he explained, "our family lived in northwest Mississippi, best cotton belt there is, plenty of rain in the winter and spring, but a sizzling inferno all summer. Great for cotton! But if you knew Mississippi summers, you'd know what Minnetonka and that fine hotel meant to our parboiled family.

"Why, I never struck anything as cool as that Hotel St. Louis," continued the judge. "Some magic about that climate, too—it gave us appetites like yearlin' calves. We could have put away most any sort of eats. But say, I never had such 'stomach bustin' vittles' in all my life. Now and then somebody'd go off hunting and bring home a load of canvasback ducks, enough for the whole crowd. Ever eat canvasbacks? Now, there's something! Can't understand those cooks; say, if we brought in enough fish just for our table, they'd fry them. Gulf fish? Shucks! nothing like your bass and pike; but no pickerel, please—too bony."

After a glass of water and a little rest, he resumed. "That hotel was like a great private mansion. Man never threw together under one roof more of the comforts of life.

"Mother liked dressing for dinner every night, too. I can see her yet all togged up fit to vamp even father. She was free evenings, 'cause Aunt Lily and Aunt Chloe took care of the younger kids and put 'em to bed. Evenings father and mother and we older children would go driving. We'd brought our coachman and horses and carriage up with us. Beautiful country around your lake, and your hills were new to us—no hills in Mississippi.

"Your nights up there beat everything. Many a night I've stood on one of those hotel verandas watching the moon rise—first brushing its light across the stars, then throwing it down on the lake in sheets of silver. Those Minnetonka nights made me feel downright religious; maybe, though, all that was just getting me ready for—" The judge stopped short.

"No, I'm not going to tell you about Clarabel. She came to Hotel St. Louis later that season with her folks. All I'll say is this: her eyes were Texas bluebonnets, her cheeks were your pink wild roses, and her hair was the sunset gold flung across your lake at evening."

Seeing the question in my face, he concluded, "Oh, yes! we were married half a dozen years later, thank the Lord."

After a brief rest, Judge Weatherby roused himself. "Tell me —after they wrecked the hotel, what then?"

He seemed relieved when I told him of the stately mansion erected on that very spot by Walter Douglas of the Quaker Oats Industry and of how happily he had lived there until his heroic death on the Titanic. The judge bade me explain. All there was to tell was simply that Mr. Douglas kept helping the women and children into the lifeboats until there was no escape for him. He went down with the iceberg-shattered Titanic.

There was silence, then the judge said, "A man who had lived in such a spot on your lake would do a thing like that. He'd already found out what heaven was like." The judge closed his eyes; he was back on our lake again. The nurse motioned to me, and we tiptoed out.

Thousands like Judge Weatherby have enjoyed glowing memories of those days when Minnetonka sparkled with gay hotels and luxurious steamboats. Beginning in the 80's, this queen of lakes felt justified in advertising her charms. Guidebooks featuring the lake as America's greatest summer resort, with excellent hunting and fishing besides, brought an overwhelming response not only from other parts of the United States but from Britain and the Continent as well.

As hotels increased in number, advertisements increased in the shrewdness of their appeal. The enlarged Chapman House came into favor during the 90's. Its neighbor on the Upper Lake, the Bartlett Place, shared with it excellent fishing grounds, which both hotels faithfully advertised. But the Bartlett Place added into favor during the 90's. Its neighbor on the Upper Lake, the fort without being compelled to be in full dress at all hours, this place will be ideal."

The Palmer House, from its high perch on the Upper Lake opposite Crane Island, sent out a call to hay-fever patients and to sportsmen desirous of hunting and fishing. Athletes and ball teams also were assured of a royal welcome.

The Mix Hill House on St. Albans Bay advertised itself as a health house with "Wholesome food, plenty of breeze and a free concert by the Mix Family Orchestra at dinner every night."

The Arlington, a large rambling house of comfort for 150 guests, picturesquely located in Wayzata, drew its share of contented guests who boasted of its menus and its home-like atmosphere.

Hotel days were days of prosperity for villagers who kept their wares before their fellow citizens and guests with such advertisements as these:

> W. B. Jones, Excelsior, keeps constantly on hand: "Dry goods, blackberries, boots, dried and canned fruit, shoes, lime, oranges, cement and lemons, brick, fresh fruits, crockery, bananas and glassware."

> H. H. Hunt, Teacher Piano, Organ, Vocal Music. Terms: 50 cents per lesson of one-half hour.
> Summit House, Excelsior.

> M. J. Guild — "Millinery and Fancy Goods. Bring on your old hats — old bonnets and hats made over to look good as new."

> Walter Phillips — "Agent for the Goodrich self-heating, self-folding bath tub."

> Mexican Mustang Liniment: "Long tested pain killer for housewife, farmer and raiser of any sort of animals. You will need it very day for the children!"

Part III — THE LAST HOTELS

At the close of World War I, only six of Minnetonka's hotels were still functioning, standing at the tail end of the great parade of hostelries that had helped make our lake famous. Of these only the Sampson House in Excelsior is still carrying on. The Keewaydin Hotel in Cottagewood, the La Paul of Excelsior, and the Del Otero at Spring Park succumbed to fire. The White House,

Excelsior, was wrecked. Part of Edgewood on the Upper Lake still survives.

THE KEEWAYDIN HOTEL, COTTAGEWOOD. Recently a quiet crowd stood looking at "Minneapolis 42 Years Ago," a display in a department store window. One of the spectators, an elderly man, was suddenly overcome with delight. He rapped sharply on the window with his cane. "Look at it! By George, Judy, just look at it!"

"Look at what, Grandpa?"

"Do you see that little old hotel there with that big tree in front of it? Say, if we hadn't got there just in the nick of time, your grandmother would have given me the mitten for sure!"

"What do you mean, Grandpa? What mitten?"

"Well, in my day when a young woman turned down a young man flat, we said she'd 'given him the mitten.' That's what your grandmother was going to do. We'd been married a year, and I'm afraid I hadn't succeeded very well as a husband. Don't know yet how I got her to come west to Lake Minnetonka with me instead of going home to her mother.

"We put up at this Keewaydin Hotel. Yes, ma'am! Your grandmother and I had the time of our lives right there in that little old hotel. Good things to eat, too, raised right in the hotel garden, and plenty of chickens and eggs and fresh milk besides. Colored waiters gave us tiptop service.

"Molly and I were a couple of kids again; fishing, picking wild berries in the woods, and dancing by moonlight on board the big boats."

"And the 'mitten,' Grandpa. What about that 'mitten'?"

"Shucks," laughed the old man with the cane, "guess your Grandmother must have lost it somewhere round that hotel. Great little old hotel, that!"

LA PAUL HOTEL, EXCELSIOR. Our Kansas wheat-belt cousin Sam had a warm spot in his heart for this hotel, which once stood not far from the present Tonka Theater. Sam had helped his widowed mother raise enough wheat to put him through college. Then he got himself a job and a bride. He had known for years where he was going to spend his honeymoon.

Minnetonka Story

Years before in the Kansas City *Star,* Sam had read the Sampson House "ad" which described Lake Minnetonka as the honeymooners' paradise.

The Sampson House was not expecting Sam; it was full. Too bad! But there was the La Paul not far away. Brussels carpets, electric lights, bellhops, excellent food turned out by three chefs, friendly companions, and plenty of "yellow jackets" (streetcar boats) formed a bright setting for the beginning of married life.

EDGEWOOD HOTEL, UPPER LAKE. Down in Monterrey, Mexico, live the grandchildren of six English steel magnates who never failed to bring their families north for the summer to Edgewood Hotel. By the time they arrived in the middle of June, they had already had three months of infernal heat and looked all "petered out."

At first they poked around, almost dazed, as though it couldn't be true: the cool breezes; the welcome shade; the clean, soft beds; the tomatoes, sweet corn, and crisp vegetables. They had never dreamed of such cool, juicy things as came out of the John Christian garden.

For the first few days, those English children out at play turned over stones and old chunks of wood with caution—there might be a centipede or a tarantula or a scorpion hiding there. As soon as they realized they had come to God's country, they relaxed, and life began in earnest. There were no servants around now, so parents played with their children. Together they swam and rowed and fished and called the neighbor's ducks which came in close formation for their handfuls of grain. There was a lot of fun around Edgewood in the good old summer time.

THE WHITE HOUSE, EXCELSIOR. The White House, dating back to '72, operated as a hotel until 1921. For the next seven years the Minnetonka Woman's Club owned and operated this building as a Community House. From 1928 until its recent sale in '46, it served as the Minnesota State Sunshine Home for the Aged. The White House has since been torn down.

Something of interest once happened on top of the White House porch. One afternoon in the 90's, a young lad climbed to its roof. Hundreds of times before he had done that very thing, but today was different. Today he had brought along scratch paper and two pencils. Today he wanted to be alone. Not likely though—with so many guests around, somebody would be sure to want him to run some errand or other.

Any minute a crowd of modish men and beruffled ladies might open that porch door and walk right out to share his perch with him. And those "Gibson girls" with their outrageous pompadours and their everlasting chatter—the next boat race, the next dance, or something or other. He was tired of folks around. He wanted to be alone to concentrate. He had a reason, a big reason.

This teen-age gentleman had heard that before pinning the mind down to high-powered effort, one should allow oneself a period of rest and relaxation. So he yawned comfortably and allowed his thoughts to idle at will.

He began to wonder how things had looked to Grandmother and Grandfather Jenkins when they first came out from Indiana in a covered wagon. A great trip—it took forty days. His folks still talked about Grandma's courage through it all. But then she was a Sherman, wasn't she? A cousin of General Sherman's ought to have courage. Hadn't Sherman helped win the Civil War?

Yes, sir! it must have taken a lot of courage to put all their hard-earned cash into the north wing of this hotel. After the north wing came the whole front, and last of all, the ell. This had been the Jenkins House, the Simpson House, and now the White House.

Then a great thought came to this lad: this White House was actually a monument to the grit and gumption of his forbears. It had been a family project. It was a success. By George, he was proud of it!

From his roof perch he looked out across the lake with new vision. He seized pencil and paper and wrote what he saw on Minnetonka. That essay won the prize offered by the Minneapolis *Journal*, a neatly framed picture which the prize winner presented to the Excelsior High School.

The late Elmer Bardwell won that prize.

HOTEL DEL OTERO, SPRING PARK. Without question, Hotel del

Minnetonka Story

Otero possessed qualities which offered special appeal to southern families. It became a tradition with these families that kept coming year after year from Dixie, as their grandparents had done years before.

In 1887, James J. Hill built this big friendly house on a point of land to get the lake breezes from all sides. All summer long, guests found it cool and refreshing.

The last proprietor, Mr. King, succeeded in keeping life at Hotel del Otero smooth, unruffled, languid, and unhurried. In its gardens grew vegetables and berries for the table; beyond an attractive lawn lay the lake inviting guests to swim or bathe or boat. The nearby hall offered opportunity to bowl or dance or play games.

Del Otero left little to be desired. When this northern Mecca was destroyed by fire July 16, 1945, its loss left a feeling of emptiness in many a heart.

THE SAMPSON HOUSE, EXCELSIOR. The only hotel remaining as a reminder of Minnetonka's heyday is the Sampson House. Leroy Sampson was a natural-born hotel keeper who looked and acted the part. In early days, he bought the Slater House, operating it efficiently until it burned down. On the same site, in '96, he erected the present Sampson House.

Fortunately, this last Minnetonka hotel commemorates in its name a man who was more than a hotel keeper. Leroy Sampson was a specialist in the joy of living. From the day his first guests arrived by stagecoach to his last day as host, Mr. Sampson's greatest pleasure was seeing his clients well-fed and happy. He enjoyed making new friends while keeping the old ones. Whenever romances sprang up among his guests, Mr. Sampson was eager to aid and abet, if he approved. However, his kindly intervention saved many an eligible man from the matrimonial trap set by some conniving dame of questionable age. He enjoyed taking his guests on fishing trips; with him along, they would catch fish. He had the "know-how."

This landmark hotel still reflects the hearty good cheer of Leroy Sampson, whose grandson Webb Sampson is its present proprietor.

| CHAPTER IX | *Foreign Guests* |

Part 1 – A FRENCH GUEST AT LAKE VIEW HOTEL

"MASHED eggs in water glasses! Pepper on them at that. Pepper on mashed eggs! *Mon Dieu, quelle soupe!*"

The nattily dressed young Frenchman seated at the breakfast table had suddenly forgotten his habitual, polite silence. "*Garcon!*" he hailed one of the waiters. "*Pardon*, bring me a hard-boiled egg in an egg cup—and *no* pepper. *Merci beaucoup!*"

Until that morning, the handsome Frenchman had remained politely quiet. The other guests at the breakfast table suddenly felt a new interest in life: what might be going to happen now?

After some time, the waiter returned. "Sorry, sir, but we haven't any egg cups in this hotel, not one, sir." The young Frenchman rose impetuously, as though about to leave the table in disgust. Like a flash the waiter met the emergency. Looking squarely into the frowning face of the disgruntled patron, the waiter rippled off a little French verse which ended:

"......... *enfant gâte,*
Voulez vous du pâte?"

It was something about a spoiled child wanting pie.

The Frenchman at first showed surprise upon hearing his mother tongue, even though tinged with an American accent; then he burst into a ringing laugh. "*Mon ami,*" he cried, reaching for the waiter's hand, "shake, as you Americans say. And now, just for this, bring me two hard-boiled eggs! Bring them in the milk pail or the dishpan, suit your own convenience." Then, in a low tone, "Look under my plate after breakfast."

That egg incident resulted in making Monsieur Philippe the

favorite at his table, and, needless to say, of the waiters as well. His careful English, adorned with his French accent, was irresistible, especially when he tried to understand the bill of fare.

That was in 1870. France was already knee-deep in the Franco-Prussian War, and young Philippe was marking time till the pain in his chest should leave him. Then he could reenter military service. That pain had brought him from Paris to America, and, heeding his physician's advice not to tarry on the Atlantic seacoast, he had struck inland with the "hope of finding things wild." Here at Minnetonka he declared he had found what he had wanted—everything, that is, but wine!

"It is the wine that I miss," he once remarked. "How can you Americans manage without wine? This, however, will greatly please *ma chère mère*; she is an ardent disciple of your Frances Willard. When my pain leaves me, my mother will say, 'Good, no wine makes it go!' Never shall I be able to convince her to the contrary.

"You do not have wine, but, *mon Dieu*, you have everything else. My people at home will never believe all the things that you have to eat. This morning were we not served chopped ham in our omelet? Extravagance! Were we not served hollowed-out melons with a block of ice therein? Luxury, unheard of luxury—the ice, I mean. And what have we for dinner but excellently roasted duck, wild duck; and for our third meal, shall we not have fish, perhaps, beautifully browned? But the wines, the relishes, the sauces, well perhaps you do not need them here in this country."

At times when he looked out across the water, he would exclaim that Lake Minnetonka was Swiss in its beauty. "Ah," he would continue, "if we had your lake in France, *mon Dieu*, we would make it useful as well. We would build upon its shore a great academy of natural science. Look at your birds, butterflies, wild life, and fish besides—endless material for laboratory work—endless!"

Some such statement as this was sure to act as a tonic for all guests at the table. Hardly could they await their turn to tell of the discoveries they themselves had made in woods and fields or while out rowing.

In fact, around that intelligent young Frenchman revolved a pleasant little world of social and intellectual intercourse. This little world showed active interest in his gradual recovery. With quiet rowing and walking and sunshine by the hour, his chest pain was slowly disappearing. Add to that the hotel's wholesome, appetizing "salt-rising" bread, wild strawberries, cream, milk, vegetables, and all the rest, and it is little wonder that one morning Monsieur Philippe's chair was empty. His pain had gone, and so had he.

France had need of all her sons; the young Frenchman had hastened to her assistance, leaving behind him a queer, empty feeling. For weeks the Lake View mourned his going, until one day a large box marked "Handle with Care" arrived. Inside were ten dozen egg cups and a card upon which were these significant words: *"Pour mon retour"*—but he never returned.

Part II – AN ENGLISHMAN ON THE MINNETONKA MENUS OF 1879

"To a man whose days and nights are absorbed in the hard labor of thinking, his retreat into holiday life in the bloom of the year is a matter of great moment. Likewise his holiday appetite becomes a matter of increasing importance. To such a man, if he live in the States, I should recommend this Minnetonka region. To my fellow countrymen I offer the same recommendation with a sigh of gratitude that I am already here.

"Here I find aristocrats from the professional and business circles of America's great cities and a few from the Continent as well. Fine chaps—interesting in conversation. Yesterday, a dozen of us turned vagabond for a day in the woods. Finer trees can not be found even in the Mother Country, than grow around this lake. When we sat down on Indian mounds to rest, our American friends spun tall yarns about the redskins.

"Hot? These Americans do not realize that Minnesota lies in the tropics, but I swear it does. Under heat, we Britishers suffer and grow surly; the Americans simply sweat, and the more they sweat, the more cheerful they get. Infernally queer, I say. Late afternoon we started home, wilted and wet from the heat but with our hands full of wild flowers for the ladies and with our faces full of smiles, for had we not been walking through paradise?

"Our appetites increased in geometric proportion as the remaining distance to our hotel decreased. We began to surmise what the evening menu might prove to be. Unlike most things in life, the realization of that meal far exceeded its anticipation. The meat course? Cock prairie chickens, a complete novelty to me, exquisite eating; with them came potatoes and gravy, no lumps! American gravy is smooth and golden. How do they manage it?

"Among the dishes that followed came many kinds of vegetables; a squash not unlike our vegetable marrow, only richer. The new beans and peas were excellent. The wild strawberries gathered in the woods here around this lake surpass anything I have ever sampled in the fruit line. Our last course was short cake dressed thick with these strawberries and submerged in cream. I confess it was difficult not to appear impolitely greedy after doing a day in the woods with only a small pocket lunch.

"Breakfast is a hearty meal on Lake Minnetonka. The wheaten bread is good; the corn flour and buckwheat cakes most excellent. Many men commence breakfast with a whole melon with ice filling the center. When our breakfast weather is 80° and going up, I do not care to try such an experiment.

"Breakfast eggs are soft-boiled, they look a positively indecent mess. The variety of fish is great and excellently cooked, with strange little relishes to pour over if one is so inclined. Beef and mutton are not as good as ours, a bit too fresh, I fancy.

"Apples here are below par. Someone tells me of a spiritualist in this locality that is a wonder at breeding fruit suited to this climate; he has a Bible name, Gideon, I believe. I hope he may take the apple under consideration and meet with success.

"The American ladies have a 'sweet tooth.' Little jugs of syrup are on every table for the ladies to pour over hominy cakes or buckwheat cakes. This 'sweet tooth' together with hot rolls and pies may account for the sallow, dyspeptic complexions of some of the ladies, otherwise charming.

"I may say in passing that American ladies are possessed of an astounding curiosity. They ask anybody anything, not for the sake of idle gossip, I find, but simply for information. They are eager to know the very things that our women would feel did not concern them. Again, American women are far more given to being modish, and 'in style all the while' than our English women. Perhaps this is not a fault. On the whole, I repeat, I find this country's women truly charming.

"In American diet I do not observe many peculiarities worth noting, except in the use of fruit jell. In Britain, we consider one teaspoonful of jelly a complete dessert in itself. Here, in these Minnetonka hotels, the guests literally plaster jell on bread, rolls, biscuits, even crackers; no thought of saving it for dessert.

"So much delicious grape jell led me to inquire as to where the grapes grow around this lake. I was told the woods are full of wild grapes and that tame grapes also are being raised with considerable success on long sloping hills a few miles to the northeast of Excelsior.* If this be true, Minnetonka hotels can continue to serve grape jell.

"In conclusion, I stoutly affirm that every meal is a feast put on the table in most tasteful manner and with perfect cookery. Such feasts have use beyond mere passing enjoyment, they bring the conviction that life in America is good, very good."

(NOTE: This English friend of my father planned to revise and publish the above before returning to England in 1880. Whether or not he succeeded in so doing, I am unable to say.)

Part III — MINNETONKA AS A GERMAN SAW IT

Nosing about in the Minnesota Historical Society Building is enough fun in itself, but coming upon unexpected treasure rouses real excitement. A couple of years ago in the reading room on the first floor, a neatly bound book came to my attention: *"Ein*

*This locality later became known as Vine Hill.

Minnetonka Story

Streifzug durch den Nordwesten Amerika," written in diary form by Herr N. Mohr.

Leafing casually through the book my attention was caught by these words: *"Am* Lake Minnetonka, Hotel Lafayette, *Sonntag*—September 2, 1883." To come suddenly upon a foreigner's estimate of our lake and of our American people was a pleasant experience. The following literal translation, beginning on page 80 of his book, simply rearranges the writer's material.

Herr Mohr starts to describe the lake and the hotel, and gets well under way when he is suddenly overwhelmed by so many things of interest, or by the frequent arrivals of new guests for the banquet to be held the next evening, *Montag,* September 3, that he loses his train of thought. Without damage to the content, I have tried in this translation to keep his train on the track. Printed in Berlin, in '84, this book had a tremendous sale in the "Vaterland."

> "On Lake Minnetonka
> Hotel Lafayette
> September 2, 1883
> On Sunday

"Has anything like our trip out west ever occurred either in ancient or modern days? Now, for the first time the whole crowd is together which on the invitation of the Northern Pacific Railway Company, through Mr. Villard, has been on hand to travel westward free of charge from the Atlantic for thousands of miles, and to take part in the celebration of the *completion* of that Northern Pacific Road which binds Portland, Oregon, to New York City by way of Chicago and St. Paul.

"How great that group of guests will be by tomorrow night, the date of the banquet, I can only surmise. Evidently those present are already three hundred in number. Thus far, all of us travel with every imaginable comfort. Upon the train, we have a bedroom at night where we had a sitting room during the day. We also have a washroom, dressing room, kitchen and storeroom upon the train along with us. What comes out of the kitchen and storeroom is bewildering, unbelievable!

"Today we are not traveling. We have a holiday out here on Lake Minnetonka. A holiday, to wander about like children out of school! To remain one whole beautiful day in one place, with the only interruption a steamboat ride, *that* is something unusual! Forever

76

would I remain here on lovely Lake Minnetonka! It is beautiful beyond compare.

"Where Lake Minnetonka lies will be difficult for you, my Berlin-ers, to understand. If you have never heard of Lake Minnetonka before our travelogue brings it to your ear, you need not offer any reproach to the insufficiency of your geographical knowledge. Neither Appleton, the American 'Baedecker,' nor the 'Guidebook for Englishmen' describes Lake Minnetonka and Hotel Lafayette, although the latter claims only one rival among the countless hotels which serve the Americans at 'watering places.'

"Lake Minnetonka and Hotel Lafayette will from this day on be renowned, for it is assembling about itself a company which attracts the gaze of the whole United States. To explain to you where the inland sea of Minnetonka lies, notice on the map in your Stieler's *Atlas* that it lies twelve English miles from Minneapolis to the south, a half hour's journey.

"The shores rise gently from the lake, which is quite enclosed by forests and cornfields. Steamboats make pleasure trips upon it. I have in my hotel office a small writing about Lake Minnetonka, well stated. Whenever you ask me later, I shall tell you more. At present, I plan to spare you my poetic outpourings, which I would have to state in prose.

"Consequently, I shall endeavor to furnish you with a likeness to this lake not far from where you live by saying that you Berlin-ers will find Havel Lake a counterpart of Lake Minnetonka. Our enthusiastic guide assures us that in all the Northwest, Minnetonka is without a rival. 'So far has its reputation penetrated, that no artist's brush, no writer's pen can adequately represent its manifold charms,' so he claims.

"The correctness of this statement, I shall not deny. To the contrary, I shall gladly concede that Lake Minnetonka is surpassingly charming, even if seldom shown upon the map. It has so many inlets and bays, islands and peninsulas, straits and isthmuses, that an immense ancestral estate could be amply furnished with them.

"The shores are handsomely wooded. Hotels and villas in every bay, half-covered with trees, speak to us, and seem to invite us in, as we pass. This lake belongs to the countless bodies of water which make up Minnesota's lake region. Upon one island, Germans from St. Paul have built themselves a charming place, where, far from the tumult of the world, they can drink a good glass in peace.

"Our hotel, Lafayette, is truly built upon American lines — four stories high, 900 feet long, and 100 feet deep. Around this charming edifice runs a remarkable veranda in Queen Anne's style, well roofed to protect us from the sun's heat. On the first floor are the conversation room, the 'parlor,' they call it, and also the dining room. In the upper stories, through the middle of the building runs a long hall, rooms lie along each side of this hall. This gigantic building is high and airy, commanding a magnificent view of the lake on different sides.

"A frame building it is, a simple neat hotel, without useless filigree. Its rooms are of unheard-of dimensions, its windows numerous, and its roofs of prodigious extent. It reminds me of some tremendous edifice for a national music carnival, or for the purpose of a long-range rifle club. Here at Hotel Lafayette, as everywhere in America, the beds are remarkably excellent. My sleep is the sleep of an untroubled infant.

"This hotel's walls are rough-cast with plaster, not painted. The furniture is neat and suitable. In hot sunshine and warm weather, this roomy, cool hotel makes a wholly friendly impression upon one. How many guests could be accommodated here, I cannot even surmise.

"Tomorrow night, September 3, there will be a great banquet here at Hotel Lafayette, to which vast numbers are invited in celebration of this Northern Pacific's completed road. Ex-president Grant arrived this morning with a swarm of politicians of every sort, present and past senators, envoys, members of Congress, governors, and so forth.

"Our own German group gained strength in Chicago by receiving into its number Messrs. Lasker, also Adolph Meier of St. Louis, also our German consul Feigel, former ambassador to Madrid. Tomorrow, after a tremendous celebration in St. Paul and Minneapolis, the Villard party will arrive here at Minnetonka. Herr Villard is the great American who has superintended the Northern Pacific's construction and brought it to completion.

"Our own German Emperor, also Baron von Bismarck were invited to this celebration, but both are represented here by the envoys, Herr von Eisendecker and Earl Lippe-Weissenfeldt. Present are envoys from Sweden, Norway, and Denmark, also the Earls Bildt and Bille.

"Along with Ex-president Grant, a large number of generals also have arrived: General Fairchild, General Baker, General MacFerly and General Hagen. I do not know many of the governors, but there are plenty of them here. This morning I met Mr. Teller, Secretary of the Interior. In this republican country such men are addressed by the title 'honorable,' therefore, Hon. Mr. Teller! Hon.

Herr Pullman, owner of a network of railroads, is here in company with Banker Schneider of Chicago.

"Out on the beautiful lawn overlooking Lake Minnetonka, I see from my window Lord Carrington in earnest conversation with Lord Onslow. At a little distance from them, Hon. James Bryce, the historian, has 'button-holed' Dr. Burchhardt from Manchester. They are engaged in constant conversation, hardly noting the glory of the sunset over the lake that lies still as a sheet of flaming glass. President Arthur, chief executive of these United States, is expected tomorrow.

Tuesday, Sept. 4, 1883
Early in the Morning

"Everything swims before my eyes this morning as I try to recall the splendor of last night's banquet — flags, flowers, and little shields at each place. And the tables, *ach Himmel!* never shall I see such long tables again during my life's span! My hand goes lame at the faintest endeavor to describe such a banquet.

"What a sight; *Gott sei Dank!* There sat the talented and distinguished of the world, with wives, daughters, and sweethearts, ladies charming in the fullest sense of the word! And the food! *Gott steh' uns bei!* I cannot explain the menu, all I know is that it was exquisitely served and wholly satisfying.

"This, my friends, was the first and the last meal I shall ever have the honor of eating with the President of this great American commonwealth. Furthermore, our intimacy has gained nothing thereby. He has not the least knowledge in the world of my existence while I, alas, shall never be able to extricate my humble self from the entanglements of the bewitching charms that his personality unconsciously cast about me.

"I imagined that the head of the United States Government would sit in the very center of the table of honor. With sidelong glances I watched the young man seated at the center. A strange disappointment rose up in me, because of his extreme youth. I asked myself why so great a nation should choose so young a man as its executive.

"Suddenly someone proposed a toast to President Arthur. I looked quickly to see the young man rise to respond. He remained seated. I had been mistaken; the situation was clear, as soon as the man on his left arose.

"President Arthur, rising to his full height, stood looking around over all the tables in quiet dignity. He was *not* so young. His manner was modest, cultured, distinguished. In fitting words he thanked us for our deafening applause, then skilfully directed our complete attention to Hon. Mr. Villard, who, said the President, is the central figure of this notable occasion.

"President Arthur made a lasting impression upon his hearers, upon myself in particular – an impression which shall remain with me. By way of explanation, the young man I had mistaken for the President was the Mayor of St. Paul.

"Former Secretary of State, Hon. Mr. Evarts, I shall never quite forget. A master of English he is, yet I lost much of what he had to say. His easily flowing language was constantly covered by screams of laughter. Over his face played a mischievous smile; even though I was unable to hear him, his face, at least, was most entertaining. Ex-president Grant is no speaker; his voice is weak, and yet he never seems in the mood to pass up a chance to speak!

"And now, I must bid farewell to this beautiful lake and thank the committee on management for the most wonderful of banquets. The other guests are packing; I must hasten! As we steam onward, I shall grieve at parting from my lovely new friend, Lake Minnetonka."

CHAPTER X	*Steamboat*
	Days

Back in the days when Rome was young, there was a Roman pleasure resort on Lake Tiberias (the Sea of Galilee). According to the historian Josephus, Galilean hills were crowned with hotels and the lake was dotted with gay gondolas. Young people loitered and loved; Cupid was busy. In Josephus' story there is only one discordant note, which the historian calls "one of Nature's cruel moments."

He explains that, back in the valley of those Galilean hills, squalls are born which sweep across the lake like whirling demons. One day, such a squall seized a Roman praefect's gondola, tossed it up like an eggshell, then dropped it with a force that sent it to the bottom of the lake where it remained. "And," remarks Josephus, "thus did the praefect's entire family cross the River Styx together."

"Nature's cruel moment" came Minnetonka's way in 1885, even though the world had stepped far enough ahead to replace the gondola with the steamboat. On a hot July day, the twelfth, a squall developed back of Spirit Knob. In the path of that whirling dervish—perhaps some eighty rods southwest of the Knob—the little steamer, *Minnie Cook*, was seized, capsized, and sunk, never to rise again. Not a Roman official and his family this time, but a former mayor of Minneapolis, his family and friends, were the ones marked as victims.

Ex-mayor and Mrs. A. C. Rand; their children Mary, Harvey, and Frank; their friends, Mr. and Mrs. Coykendall and daughter Kittie; another young friend, Robert Hussey; and George McDonald, the engineer—all ten, as a result of that squall, crossed the River of Death together. The Rand disaster remains to this day Minnetonka's supreme tragedy.

The drowning disaster in Josephus' Latin story is the only highlight in his narrative, but if .those old Romans had had steamboats to play with, they would have had fifty-seven varieties of excitement: unfortunate launchings, boiler blowups, landing smash-ups, rash speculation, violent competition, *et cetera*.

Without steamboats, Minnetonka could never have had a golden age; with steamboats, our lake climbed from dim obscurity into the light of dazzling fame. The steam-navigation era was ushered in by the Rev. Charles Galpin, an all-round man who was spiritually minded, money minded, and politically minded as well. As soon as he had turned over his spiritual flock to their new shepherd, the Rev. Charles Sheldon, he was foot-loose and Scot free to meet the material needs of the community and of his own lean purse.

A steamboat covered the needs of all concerned. As to its name, the ex-preacher had a happy thought. Why not bind this lake and its future to the rest of the Minnesota commonwealth by christening the new steamer the *Governor Ramsey?* Graceful gesture! Proud as Punch, Governor Ramsey himself came to visit his namesake and to try out her merits.

Compared with the fine river boats plying the Mississippi and Ohio at that time, the *Governor Ramsey* looked like a dinky little thing, but to lake people that fifty-foot side-wheeler meant more than they could well express. From 1855 to 1868, the *Governor* carried every sort of supply from bootjacks, buttons, and thread to lumber, wheat, flour, and furniture. Squeezed in among these necessities of life were all the passengers that could find foot room.

In 1868, the *Sue Gardiner* came to keep the *Governor Ramsey* company. On that boat, R. T. Mann began his steamboat career. Like his father and brothers, Tom Mann preferred water to land.* After serving the *Clyde, Lotus, Hattie May* and *Saucy Kate* as pilot, he was given the rank of captain. Captain R. T.

*Young Tom and his big brother Oscar ran the *Sue Gardiner* from the day she was launched and for many years after their father John Mann had purchased her.

Mann retired from the steamboat business in 1922, twenty-one years before his death.

Charles May entered the steamboat picture in 1870. Mr. May was head of a grist mill in Excelsior, owner of another mill and a hotel on St. Albans Bay, as well as manager and owner of the Excelsior stave and barrel-head factory. He planned to invest the profits from these enterprises in steamboats.

His handsome, speedy *May Queen* was hailed with delight by an increasing number of tourists, but that very first season, her boiler burst, bringing death to the engineer. The *Katie May*, a luxurious craft with closed cabin, was Mr. May's second steamboat. Her boiler also exploded, taking toll of three lives. The *Katie May* was repaired and renamed *Saucy Kate*.

Charles May began to study and investigate various makes of engines. The field of mechanics was pitifully limited in those days, but he canvassed the situation thoroughly. From 1874 to 1881, he had a fine fleet of steamers equipped with engines that stood up and boilers that did not burst.

Those who could not make the May steamers boarded Major Halstead's *Mary*, a 78-foot propeller, the largest steamboat on the lake in 1880. The *Mary* rapidly grew in favor, especially with the guests of Hotel St. Louis. On the first of July, 1880, while she waited at the dock of that hotel, her boiler exploded, killing three and injuring eight.

Those blowups might have given steam navigation on our lake a black eye, but there was no time to brood over past misfortunes. The future was more important. Minnetonka, like Uncle Remus' rabbit, just had to climb now—twenty thousand guests a year were after her. They came by families with loads of trunks to spend the season in her hotels and on her steamboats.

By 1880, seventeen big hotels—including many of the first hotels greatly enlarged—were perched atop the hills around the lake. Their guests clamored for boat rides. A forty-five mile steamboat ride was especially popular on a hot summer day. More steamboats were needed every season. Charles May's freighter, the *Rambler*, had for several years relieved passenger boats from carrying supplies. On this freighter, George Hopkins began his lake career as engineer. He delivered supplies to hotels, to boarding houses, and even to farmers along the shore.

Minnetonka's greatest need in the face of the incoming tide of visitors was steamboats—still more steamboats! People in Minneapolis and St. Paul—even in Chicago—began to see a fortune in a steamboat. They began to talk, to plan, to borrow money, to write East for capital.

Business boomed, train loads of boilers, engines, and parts began to arrive at Wayzata. Some of the material remained in the Wayzata boat works with the builder William Crump; some went to Sawin Dyer, in Excelsior.

Excitement, competition, and speculation flourished around the lake during the 70's. Returning guests found bigger, handsomer, and better equipped steamers each season. For pleasure-seekers, the steamboat business meant entertainment, but for investors it meant perplexity of mind and a drain on the purse, for a time at least.

Styles in steamboats changed as rapidly as women's fashions. Many a man, after seeing his dream materialize into a graceful steamboat, was sure to hear of a better make of engine or of some new-fangled equipment. He had no peace of mind until he could make the change. This took money.

Now and then, Charles May came out with a surprise package —for instance, the *Hattie May*, the first stern-wheeler on Lake Minnetonka. To outdo the *Hattie May*, the *Lotus* came out three years later, in 1881. She was a queer freak devised to secure speed. Two high-pressure engines applied their combined force to the same revolving shaft with the desired result—the *Lotus* shot across the water. Excitement ran high. Daring passengers kept the *Lotus* busy every hour of the long summer days and far, far into the night.

The *Lotus* belonged to the Lake Minnetonka Navigation Company which came into the steamboat picture in 1880 with one small steamer, the *Nautilus*. Gradually this company bought up steamboats and repaired, revised, and returned them to compete with free enterprise upon the lake.

James J. Hill dabbled in the steamboat business long enough

to put out, in '79, a forty-foot propeller tugboat named the *Seventy-Six*. For the next twenty-seven years, this little craft underwent continual revision. Every time it was overhauled it came back under a new name, ending its career, in 1906, as the *Casino*, the last steamboat to rival streetcar boats, the "yellow jackets."

One steamboat, the *W. D. Washburn* owned by Charles May, had been fitted up with two engines. To go ahead with one while reversing with the other would enable the *Washburn* to turn around on a postage stamp. Returning to Excelsior from its trial trip, both engines insisted on going head on, splintering the dock and the *Washburn* too. Repaired and renamed the *Mercury*, this steamboat was skidded eight miles across country and slipped into the Minnesota River to do service there.

Until 1881, Minnetonka had never seen a steamer more than a hundred feet long. With that year dawned the era of bigger boats, the *City of St. Louis* heading the list. She was a side-wheeler 160 feet long, capacity 1,000 passengers. People gasped at the beauty of this snow-white, gilt-trimmed giant with its jet black smokestacks and its paddle boxes bearing painted scenes. Her crew of thirty-two blue-uniformed men moved about through the carpeted cabins or along the sleek decks, attending to the wants of the passengers in courtly fashion. A sixty-piece band played soft dinner music, as well as lively tunes for dancing. Although a thousand passengers could be nicely accommodated, the *City of St. Louis* somehow made room for 1,750 people clamoring to see the Harlan-Teemer rowing regatta.

At that same regatta her rival, the *Belle of Minnetonka*, offering room for 2,500 passengers ordinarily, reinforced her decks to allow 3,360 souls on board for that gala occasion. Three hundred feet long, the *Belle* was the biggest vessel ever put afloat on our lake. She came with the Hotel Lafayette as part of the Jim Hill enterprise.

The *City of St. Louis* had been built at Wayzata with the exception of her hull, which was shipped here from Indiana. But the *Belle* had plied up and down the Ohio and Mississippi for years as a river boat under the name of the *Phil Sheridan*. Some uppercrust New Orleans women had so admired this big river boat that they donated their jewelry toward the purchase of a bell for it. So the *Belle of Minnetonka* not only had size to her credit, but she also inherited a bell with a clear, resonant tone. Her advent upon the lake created intense excitement, and passengers kept her busy day and night.

In racing to meet the trains pulling into Wayzata every half hour, the *Belle* was usually in the lead of the *City*. Then came the *Lotus*, the *Hattie May*, the *Minneapolis*, and the rest of the lake steamers, churning the water, clanging bells, blowing whistles and burning out smokestacks with the overfiring necessary to compete with the big leaders.

There was really no need for such wasteful and dangerous haste. With passengers enough and to spare, all the boats came away from the Wayzata docks loaded to capacity. When ninety steamers got to racing madly without rhyme or reason, the Lake Minnetonka Navigation Company stepped in and bought the whole lay-out, putting an end to such foolishness.

Boats, hotels, investments, profits, losses—all combined tell only part of the story of steamboat days. Before the end of their first season here, strangers learned that each steamboat had a personality of its own, differing according to the crew. The Carman boys, the Mann brothers, James Mitchell, Herbert May, George Hopkins, George West, John R. Johnson—all captains or pilots—furnished passengers with endless topics of conversation. Ex-slave Tom Powell, fireman on the *City*, was brimming over with stories about river boats coming up from the South. Stewards like Willard Perkins and band boys like George Barton and John Seamans each in his way gave color and character to his particular boat. John Seamans, father of radio-singer Ade Seamans, delighted the passengers when he sang whatever aria they might choose.

Day after day a steamer was apt to carry about the same contented, loyal clientele. Babies fell asleep in their black mammies' arms; children romped from deck to deck; grown-ups chatted and gossiped; young people, vibrant with life and energy, burst into snatches of such songs as "Where Did You Get That Hat," "My Last Cigar," and "Putting on Style."

If the historian Josephus could have visited our lake in steamboat days, he would have found Cupid even busier here than among the Roman youths and maidens around the Sea of Galilee. Shady shores here for loitering? Yes, but our lake offered something far more alluring—moonlight dancing aboard the big steamers!

As soon as the moon turned the world to silver, the steamer's dining room would be cleared and the music would begin its delectable, dreamy, dangerous strains. Hearts beat faster, toes tingled, hands clasped—the dance was on. Away those young folks glided into a mystic, nebulous world bounded by the moon and stars above and by dark, silent water below.

One night, aboard the *Belle of Minnetonka*, an unusually gay crowd covered the dance floor, while an equally merry group of onlookers held ringside seats. Off at one side, however, sat two women appearing strangely alone and out of place. Hundreds of times they had chaperoned dances in their own private school for girls back in Brookline, Massachusetts, but here they felt utterly desolate.

To come west for the summer vacation had seemed like a mad flight for these two Jenny Wrens. New clothes had been sternly ruled out—the trip was going to cost enough anyway. Clad in scant, plain, brown lawn dresses in the midst of color, fashion, and fun, the Winfield sisters *knew* that life had passed them by. Even the moonlight seemed cold as steel. They shivered as they turned away from the festive scene before them and gazed out over the lake.

At that moment of despair, the impossible came to pass. Two men they had met the day before at Hotel del Otero were asking them for the next dance. Positively overwhelming, of course, but the Winfield sisters met the emergency by being so completely gracious in their refusal that these gentlemen sat out the entire evening in their company. A charming evening! Such beautiful moonlight!

The next morning no one could find the Winfield sisters.

Minnetonka Story

Men have their share of curiosity, and the two men in question were not only curious, but deeply concerned. With no heart now for steamboating, they struck out along country roads riding their "bone-shakers" side by side, trying to solve the mysterious disappearance of those "talented, well-educated, wonderfully fine young women."

The Winfield sisters had not gone far—only to St. Paul to be modernized: new corsets, new bustles, ruffled gowns, new shoes, new coiffures, new feather fans. After their return, the moonlight dancers had to edge over a bit to make room for two older couples of dignified, elite bearing, dressed up to the minute.

Romance had found the Winfield girls by moonlight aboard the *Belle of Minnetonka*. The following summer both couples came back to this lake for their honeymoon.

Speaking of the Winfield sisters' fluffy ruffles reminds me of what once stood behind my neighbor's kitchen door. When I first saw Mrs. Oskar Carlson's ironing board, I felt certain she had knocked out one of the partitions and had padded it to do the ironing for some giantess. The fact is young women in the 80's wore full skirts, long enough to cover their toes in front with much to spare behind. Mrs. Carlson lived only a few stones' throws from Hotel St. Louis, where there were many young ladies whose long trains and full, ruffled skirts got terribly wrinkled at every dance. A long, wide ironing board, a hot iron, and Mrs. Carlson's skillful hand solved the problem. After a visit to her house, milady could step out on the dance floor of any steamer, feeling sure there was not one offending wrinkle in all the length and breadth of her ruffled loveliness.

Old-timers around Lake Minnetonka recall those steamboat days with pride, the days that tied this little lake world to the great outside. Far away in the deep South I find people still bound to this spot by memories that grow clearer with the lapse of time. Mr. and Mrs. Bragg, of Vicksburg, are Minnetonka enthusiasts whose respective families had the habit of coming to our lake, bag and baggage, season after season.

When they learned I lived near Lake Minnetonka, Mr. Bragg began to flood me with questions. Did Excelsior still have six barns on Main Street and three more around the corner? Did I want to know who owned those barns? Had I ever heard of Orpheus Gates who kept the finest livery horses in Minnesota?

At this point Mrs. Bragg shushed up her husband, remarking that it would have been far more decent to inquire about the churches in Excelsior, especially that dear little Episcopal Chapel. Was it still standing, still being used? She was glad to hear that the chapel had been moved without a crack, in 1904, to a lovely spot among big pines just a block up a hill from Water Street, sometimes called Main Street.

Mrs. Bragg's next question concerned Hamlin Hunt who had roomed at the Summit House and had taught music at 50 cents per lesson. Although he was a mighty fine teacher, she didn't like taking piano lessons during vacation. It seemed that every time she had a lesson, Pilot Hopkins just happened to let the "kids" take the wheel and steer. One day this small musician explained to Mr. Hopkins exactly why she always lost *her* chance at his wheel—those "plaguey" music lessons were to blame!

"It's a darn shame," he declared. "Here, steer the old tub as long as you want to." Imagine calling a beautiful lake steamer an old tub! But that was Hopkins for you—a unique character, full of yarns too. He attracted children to him as surely as a magnet picks up pins.

A dozen times she heard him tell how the first minute spring came, he'd grab his hat and run right out of that bank in Minneapolis where he worked winters. Yes, sir! he'd keep right on running till he got out here "to the prettiest little pond on the globe."

Mrs. Bragg was pleased to hear that George Hopkins had run his own boat, the *Victor*, through the 1920's and then had retired to enjoy life after more than fifty years of service on Minnetonka.

Now it was Mr. Bragg's turn. As a youngster, he had watched the Narrows being dredged in '84 to allow big steamers to pass through. He was one of the first to cross over on the new cable ferry loaded with horses and buggies and a farm wagon. Of course,

Minnetonka Story

I told him about the fine steel and concrete bridge that has spanned the Narrows since 1911.

A look of pride shone in Mr. Bragg's eyes as he explained how *his* family—not his wife's—had found this lake in the first place. Minnetonka had been recommended to them by an uncle, a Confederate officer, General Braxton Bragg. In the Civil War, General Bragg had proved a gallant leader, but somehow he got cornered in Chattanooga by General Ulysses Grant. In spite of brilliant tactics and a gallant defense, Bragg was forced to surrender.

Strangely enough, according to General Bragg's nephew, barely fifteen years after the close of the war, these two generals found themselves face to face again—this time at Hotel Lafayette on Lake Minnetonka. These one-time enemies were immediately attracted to each other. A strange pair they were—the tall, elite, well-groomed Bragg with his handle-bar mustache and the stubby, tough-looking, carelessly dressed Grant with his full beard.

Every day they sat aboard a steamboat by the hour, buried deep in conversation. No matter which steamboat—they tried them all. Most often, however, they were seen on the *City of St. Louis* where the food was delicious, the service perfect, and the music the best this side of Chicago.

Perhaps nowhere else could conditions have been more perfect for fostering a growing friendship that lasted through life. These two ex-generals could, on occasion, act like school boys. When their particular steamboat shot ahead of its rivals and pulled into the Wayzata port first, they shouted themselves hoarse just for the fun of the thing. For a fortnight, these strange friends toured in and out of the bays, around the islands, and across wide stretches of quiet water, discussing how to rebuild their great country which once had all but fallen to pieces.

As soon as Mr. Bragg had finished with the generals, Mrs. Bragg wanted to hear about the Halstead brothers. She had seen the Major, but what about the Captain? Were they really queer? And was it true that lotus lilies won't grow anywhere on the lake but in their bay? And that singing Viking, John Johnson—what-

ever became of him and his big boat? And what about Minnetonka Mills? Had I ever had any flour from there?

Before I could answer, the time between trains was up. After
promising to send my answers by mail, I bade the Braggs adieu.

CHAPTER XI | Minnetonka's Mystery Men

On Halstead's Bay, Minnetonka's westernmost arm, there stood, for nearly fifty years, a house of mystery. "The Hermitage" had no neighbors except the quiet kind; the dead, asleep in their mounds nearby. Deathly silence muffled the place like a pall; a silence broken in winter by the winds moaning through bare trees, and in summer by the birds singing in joyous chorus. Winter days when the birds were gone and the winds were still, the silence within the Hermitage would have grown unbearable but for the song of a teakettle sung to the tick-tock of a clock.

No romping children ran in and out of that house at play; no busy housewife sang at her work in that kitchen; no mischievous fingers pulled books and furnishings out of place. Things remained static, year in, year out. No woman's hands ever tidied up the place. Dust accumulated and windows grew dim with fly specks and cobwebs.

The drab desolation of the Hermitage contrasted sharply with the fresh loveliness of its setting. It stood upon a little bluff, an important looking, two-story frame house with plenty of windows and a veranda besides. Like a lone sentinel, it stood guard over the gigantic trees of the Big Woods which still survive in that spot and the lotus lilies that to this day cover the sheet of water lying at the foot of the bluff. These lovely lilies are never disturbed by squalls that lash the rest of the lake to a lather, so protected in the lap of its sheltering shores lies Halstead's Bay.

On the shore of this bay was the Hermitage, the home of the two Halstead brothers. For almost half a century they lived there, but never together. One at a time, in solitude, each finished the span of his life, each in turn meeting a tragic death.

92

Both brothers were city-bred easterners, exponents of genteel living. Both bore evidence of refined and cultured surroundings during childhood days. Youth and early young manhood had evidently been devoted to broad education and travel, a fact clearly discerned by all who came to know them.

Why did these white-collar gentlemen ever come west to take up pioneer life among strangers in this raw, undeveloped, new country? Neither came with the intention of lumbering. The trees of the Halstead claim were guarded with jealous care; the owners never cleared more than the acre on which their house stood. Neither one cared to farm or mill or speculate in land. Neither man ever included hard work in his life's program.

"Every man's work," according to George Eliot, "if pursued steadily, tends in this way to become an end in itself and so to bridge over the loveless chasms of life." The Halstead brothers were evidently content to keep their "loveless chasms," at least their lives were lives of ease here by the waters of Minnetonka. While living here, they met neither romance nor love. Perhaps they had already made the acquaintance of these emotions. Perhaps unrequited love had already played havoc with their hearts. No one knows.

Even today, a man who has successfully warded off Cupid's darts for years is the subject of some comment, but in those pioneer days, when Dan Cupid worked overtime—well, it just wasn't understandable. One after the other, those tall, handsome brothers chose to leave their past somewhere back East, and decided to begin life where people knew nothing of their personal history. They both walked the straight and narrow path of upright living, wholly content to meet life alone, without the solace of a helpmeet.

The early life of those two men was very nearly a closed book. Their dignified, proper secrecy enshrouded those able, clever brothers in a cloud of mystery. Who were their parents, what were their childhood experiences, what influences of education, of travel, of business, of friends, and what experiences in love had helped mold their personalities? The mystery grew in proportion as people became well enough acquainted with them to get a glimpse inside the Hermitage.

The Halstead house was literally lined with books; books in Greek, Latin, French, German, Spanish; books treating of philosophy, spiritualism, magic, mechanics, art and science; books and still more books, including all the best English and American classics.

Not only books were given a place in that home, but there was room for endless curios and souvenirs from foreign lands, such as stuffed birds from South America, mounted anteaters from Australia, strings of Japanese bells and little idols sitting demurely on shelves in front of rich tapestries. Strange furnishings for a pioneer's home!

The first Halstead to establish Minnetonka residence, in '55, was Frank, a young man of twenty-two. Now twenty-two is not very old, but Frank had already had six years in the United States Navy. One might infer that he came from a sea-faring family, because he and three brothers had already left the Atlantic and had cruised around Cape Horn, finally reaching the California coast.

Just why Frank took French leave of his brothers and struck inland, not stopping till he had reached Lake Minnetonka, and just why he started to live a solitary, a lonely life for a vigorous lad of twenty-two is still an unsolved mystery.

Neither Frank nor his brother George, who came years later, ever admitted he felt a single twinge of loneliness. "Look," each in turn exclaimed, pointing to his books, "am I not in the company of the best men and women in all the world?" Both men were intent upon studying and reading, hour after hour. Can it be that these two seamen in all their travels had seen the world from the outside only? And can it be they longed for just the sort of opportunity that life by this lake afforded them: the opportunity to study the world from the *inside* out, by means of deep reading and contemplative thinking?

It is a matter of real regret that no one was ever able to get behind either man's "curtain of consciousness." As they read and studied, what conclusions did they draw, what attitudes of mind did they entertain? What new materials did they find in books for new mental processes? Great ideas, to be of actual benefit to humankind, must be given clear, forceful expression. Did these brothers think great thoughts? If so, why were their lips sealed? That, too, must remain a mystery.

Each Halstead brother, in turn, was dubbed a hermit. By definition, a hermit is one who retires from society to some desolate spot, preferably a desert, to live in utter solitude, generally in order to reflect upon religion. In this sense, neither Halstead could have qualified as a hermit. Although not socially aggressive, each showed a definite liking for his fellow beings. No desolate desert spot had they chosen for a dwelling place; instead, they established residence on one of Minnetonka's loveliest bays. As far as religion was concerned, they left that matter to the Excelsior ministers, except once—the time Captain Frank, as justice of the peace, performed a marriage ceremony for a young German couple.

"Hermits of reverie," once remarked Mrs. Humphrey Ward, "are scared by the busy world, and find themselves out of place in action." This could not be said of the two Halsteads when the Civil War put them to the test. As soon as the War broke out they proved themselves frightened at nothing and eager for action. Both of them hurled themselves into service; Frank enlisting from the Minnetonka region and his brother George from New Jersey.

No slackers, these brothers! Their war record is enviable. Frank received a commission on the flagship *Minnesota* in an Atlantic squadron. On this same vessel, whom should he find as a comrade in arms but his older brother George! Both were soon recognized as gifted, alert, experienced seamen; the whole squadron was left in their command whenever the rear admiral was summoned to a land conference.

Together they worked like a powerful, invincible team. Together they shared the triumph of a Union victory over the Confederate forces at Hatteras Inlet. Together they held counsel over their commander; by both Halsteads, the rear admiral of their squadron was suspected of being stupid, and worse yet, disloyal to the Union. Both resigned, asking for transfers. Each

95

went his separate way, serving the Union cause till the close of
the War.

Frank Halstead became captain of the steamship *General
Pillow*, and as such, the leader of an ammunition squadron in the
Mississippi. To keep the supplies of ammunition within the reach
of the Union army and, at the same time, out of the reach of the
Confederates required daring and foresight.

One day fire broke out on the *General Pillow*. Captain Halstead kept his head. He seized a hose and worked like a mad-
man, shouting his orders and directing the work at one and the
same time. When the last spark was extinguished, his crew
cheered him till not a man could speak above a whisper.

As soon as the War was over, Captain Frank left the United
States Navy Service and returned to Minnetonka. Straightway
he began to dream of building a lake steamer. In his dreams he
always called his phantom steamboat *Mary* after the "best Mother
a boy ever had." Ten years after the close of the War his dream
came true.

One day in '76, the *Mary*, a seventy-five-foot propeller built
on graceful lines, stood ready for the launching. Her owner had
borrowed money to complete his project. Often during her construction he had felt blue enough. The debt he had incurred was
like a millstone around his neck. His spirits rose, however, when
his lovely *Mary* was about ready to take off. The day of her
launching approached. He had hard work to conceal his keen
delight—Captain Frank always had disliked any manifestation
of pride.

"I'll soon be in the clear," he kept saying to himself the morning of the eventful day. "It won't take long to pay for her if
nothing unexpected happens." The hour set for the launching
drew near. Great crowds gathered. The work of loosening the
Mary from her moorings began. And then—the "unexpected"
happened. Somehow, during the launching, the beautiful boat
suffered very severe damage before the eyes of her dismayed
owner.

Now, how could he pay back all that he had borrowed?

Stricken with grief, he hurried home—not to the comfort of a sympathizing wife, not to the diversion offered by children, but only to his books, to a cold kitchen stove, to a dust-covered table and an unmade bed. Small comfort for a man's broken heart!

Respecting his grief and thinking it best not to disturb him, Captain Halstead's neighbors refrained from calling on him the evening of that fateful day. The next morning an empty boat was discovered with its oars carefully laid inside. An empty boat and a lifeless body, found near Crane Island, closed the last life chapter of Mystery Man No. 1.

Captain Frank Halstead was laid to rest near his Hermitage. In answer to the sad news, his brother George hurried west and took over the Hermitage himself. Major George, born in 1820, was thirteen years older than his deceased brother. In spite of the difference in age, his personal resemblance to Captain Frank was disconcerting.

Like the captain, he, too, had performed brilliant military service on the staff of the fighting *Phil Kearney*. Of all his Civil War experiences, the moment when he saw Robert E. Lee surrender at Appomattox Courthouse was unquestionably the most dramatic. Major Halstead made no bones of being an ardent admirer of that great Confederate leader.

Major George hung his war medals, his canteens, his drinking cups, his tattered colors, and his faithful firearms alongside those of his departed brother. To all intents and purposes the older brother was a facsimile, an earlier installment, if you will, of the younger one. He was a greater student than Captain Frank had been; in fact, he had graduated from Princeton and had taken a course in law. Why he, too, chose to live in solitude, no one knows.

As sole proprietor of the Hermitage, he finished the last quarter-century lap of his life. There, for twenty-five years, he drank coffee alone from his 1759 coffee pot. Alone, he sat by the fireplace in his Jeff Davis chair. Alone, he listened to his French marble clock of the First Empire as it ticked off the passing of time.

Minnetonka Story

In one respect, Major Halstead differed quite noticeably from his brother. The Major mingled much more freely with people than the Captain had ever done. To tell the truth, the last proprietor of the Hermitage was definitely pleased to welcome picnickers—and also their lunch baskets.

As a tribute to his brother's memory, Major George brought the steamboat *Mary* into condition and ran her himself with all the ease and grace of an expert seaman. In '80, after three or four years of service, the *Mary* had the poor taste to blow up her boiler. The damaged boat was repaired in Excelsior by S. H. Dyer, father of the late Arthur Dyer, of Cottagewood. Then, for two years more, Major Halstead enjoyed the steamboat business and the returns therefrom. In '82, he sold the *Mary* and retired.

As age came on, the Major's mind remained as clear as a bell. French, German, Spanish, which would you prefer to hear? This scholarly man read all with equal ease. In case you might crave a passage of translation, he was ready: the Trojan War, as told in Greek by the poet Homer, or a sketch of Roman history recounted in Latin by Tacitus, or perhaps a few paragraphs from Cicero's treatise on old age, "De Senectute." He was ready to respond to any choice one might make.

In his later years, Major George might easily have been catalogued as a social favorite, according to the *Northwest Tourist*, July 18, 1885:

"Minnetonka is itself again. Major Halstead, who has made an alarmingly long absence has returned. Matrons and maids singing, 'What's this dull town to me?' have ceased their doleful dirge, and the Major has returned to enjoy his own, and is (as always) the model of high-bred chivalry. The Hermitage once more shines with his presence."

The Major was undeniably popular with women, in spite of the fact that he always wore ladies' shoes—the high, many-buttoned kind in vogue at that time.

As Major Halstead felt the weight of increasing years, he bent lower and lower under their burden. Once straight as an arrow, this old soldier now leaned farther and farther forward as though anxious to reach the goal.

One morning in September, 1901, a neighbor found the Hermitage* nothing but a heap of ashes. Major George had made the goal. He had stepped across the Great Divide. Only his ashes were left to indicate the close of the last chapter of Mystery Man No. 2.

*The site where now stands the Zumbra Heights home of Col. and Mrs. H. Terry Morrison.

CHAPTER XII	*Minnetonka*
	Milling

WHILE fine hotels and handsome steamboats were building Minnetonka's fame as a pleasure resort, flour barrels, marked "Minnetonka Mills," were introducing her name to scores of dealers in Boston, New York, Philadelphia, London, Paris, and Stockholm. To them Minnetonka meant not fun, but flour.

During the years that Minnetonka Milling was making a practical reputation for our lake, a little boy and a young bride, one after the other, enjoyed the romantic side of that enterprise.

Part I – AS A BOY SAW IT

Mrs. Perkins had felt a vague uneasiness ever since her husband had left at daybreak. He hadn't said where he was going, and now it was getting late. Tom wasn't as young as he used to be; something might have happened.

"Grandma, where is Grandpa, anyway?" At that moment two small boys saw their answer appear in the doorway, a string of fish in one hand and a bouquet of wild flowers in the other. In boisterous delight, both boys charged upon their big playmate, scattering fish and flowers over the floor.

Grandmother Perkins, relieved of anxiety for her Tom, gathered up the debris without a word and retreated to the kitchen. She'd have the fish for supper. Ed and Julia were coming after the children and they might as well stay to eat.

At supper Grandfather Perkins asked his son Ed if he'd heard the bad news about St. Anthony Falls, how the limestone ledge was being undermined by the back action of the current. Mill owners along the Falls were blue as a whetstone.

At this point, Grandfather cleared his throat. "That's the reason I went exploring today. And what do you think I found only 'bout ten miles west of here? A millpond and a dam. There used to be a sawmill there, till 'bout ten years back. The mill burned down, but the dam's all right, and the millpond's as good as ever. The dam's across Minnehaha Creek that empties out of Lake Minnetonka. There is the water power that's going to last. It's going to waste now, sure as thunder."

Grandmother Perkins stirred uneasily. Hadn't Thomas vowed he was through with the milling business when they sold their mill back in Albion, New York? Hadn't he seen that Edward didn't care for milling? Hadn't they come west for the express purpose of giving their son a chance to find something that suited him? And now—milling—milling again! She looked out the window at young Minneapolis lighting up for the evening. Nice town, growing every day; she liked it.

"Would we have to move out there?" Grandmother's voice sounded weak.

* * *

A few weeks later, in the spring of 1869, life began again for Grandfather Perkins. Thomas Hooker Perkins bought the land surrounding his future mill site, six hundred and forty acres in all. Immediately, he and his son Edward began drafting plans for the new flour mill, unaware that they were actually laying out a paradise for two small boys.

One of those boys, Willard Perkins, wrote in reminiscence: "We lived in a nice little red house on the prettiest hill you ever saw, to the south of the Minnetonka Boulevard. The hill I could find blindfolded, but now the house is gone. That house was more than home, it was heaven."

So much happened in that summer of '69 that only young eyes, capable of changing focus with lightning rapidity, could see everything that was going on. To build and equip a flour mill from scratch, and to present it to the public as a going concern by threshing time challenged the wits and skill of Thomas Perkins, despite the years of milling experience behind him. To his grandsons, that summer presented a succession of miracles. Every day brought more excitement. The sound of hammers lulled the boys to sleep at night and awakened them early in the morning. The dam was put in shape, and new houses were going up for mill hands.

Sometimes on Sunday both Perkins families rowed up Minnehaha Creek into Lake Minnetonka. What a sight! Little Willard was sure it was the biggest ocean in the world, but just the same he liked his millpond best. It was such a beautiful looking glass framed in a tangle of birch trees, bushes and vines, and edged with blue flags and cattails.

One evening Grandfather Perkins announced that the mill was done and that he was going to try out the machinery the next morning. That was a momentous occasion; both families stood waiting with little Willard perched high on Grandfather's shoulder. The great moment arrived, the power was turned on, the millstones began to turn. The machinery started to purr a strange, sweet sort of music that meant success.

In the fall of '69, T. H. Perkins' Minnetonka Mill was open for business. Wheat came from every direction, even from fifty miles away. Ox carts brought wheat, rowboats brought wheat, barges brought wheat; even the steamboat *Governor Ramsey* came down the millpond, heavy with grain for the new mill.

According to Willard Perkins: "Several neighbors would bring wheat at the same time. It would take two days to grind that wheat into flour and feed (bran and shorts). They brought their eats with them, making coffee around their campfire, but Grandfather provided a place for them to sleep."

To visit the mill was enough to make a fellow's heart beat double-quick. Why, even big boys like Fred Narimore and Fred Works froze in their tracks to see wheat turned into flour. The smell of that newly crushed wheat was the evasive fragrance of mignonette heavy with dew. White powdery dust from the flour clung to walls and rafters and roof, turning cobwebs into fairy lace. The mill hands turned white from head to foot and so did little Willard, but that was part of the fun.

If the younger Perkins boy had been told that the mill was only 44 x 33 feet and 3½ stories high, he wouldn't have been a trifle disturbed. Feeling like a worm in the dust, he gazed upon that immense pile of architecture in utter humility, sure that it must be the biggest building in the world.

It was more than size, however, that intrigued this boy; to him the mill was something human. It was a benevolent personage winking its window-eyes by moonlight and opening them wide by daylight. It was a cheery presence crooning celestial music, rain or shine. With a strange possessiveness, this child loved his mill.

Related to the chief object of his affections were other interests. Life was beautiful, especially after one added ducks, pigs, and a young lady to one's mill.

The ducks came first. They were Grandmother Perkins' answer to waste; they relished weed seed, shrivelled kernels, and lumps of moldy wheat cast off by the mill. To Willard, ducks on the pond were the prettiest, most graceful things imaginable, but on land they caused him no end of worry. Pail after pail of screenings they shovelled down into their crops without rhyme or reason. Wouldn't their bulging crops burst as they dragged along, barely missing the ground? Well, anyway, his ducks laid eggs every day.

To gather duck eggs swaying in fragile nests of reeds and water vines almost beyond a small boy's reach—ah, there was adventure for you! One day ambition overreached discretion; the small boy lost his footing. Down he went, his head striking bottom, his feet catching in a tight tangle of lily stems and pickerel weed. Luckily for him, the grip on his feet was not weeds alone; it was his brother's desperate hold. From that time on, Louis was the family hero, the life saver.

* * *

"Ducks are a lot politer, but I like pigs better anyway, don't you, Louis?" Willard observed one day.

Louis was too busy to answer. Both boys together had more than they could do to keep the hog troughs full of wet shorts for a starving, squealing, jostling pack of porkers.

In early spring, Grandfather Perkins had tucked a big bunch

of young pigs back among the hills—far away from the Minnetonka Mills settlement, out of sight or sound or smell.

The Perkins pigs were well fed—nothing like the skinny, razor-back specimens that roamed the streets of Wayzata, filching a scanty living from gardens and garbage. The miller's hogs had enough to eat, enough and to spare, because his mill was a custom gristmill. People paid for the grinding of their wheat in flour, shorts, and bran according to the amount of mill work done. Thomas Perkins barreled up his share of flour and sold it readily. Bran and shorts, however, he found hard to move—no demand, until he went into pigs.

Autumn days, which brought bulk and weight to those pigs, brought the opening of school to their caretakers. School was held at that time in the little Episcopal Chapel of St. John's, which once stood to the right of Minnetonka Boulevard leading to Minneapolis.

To young Willard, his first venture into the field of learning would have proved unbearable, but for the goddess standing at her desk in front of the church altar. That was Maggie Bartow, his first teacher, who won his heart for life. In his eyes, Maggie was every inch a queen crowned with a glory of soft, abundant hair and clad in some heavenly stuff that shimmered like sunshine. A smile from her was balm to his timid, uncertain soul.

Wondering what school was all about, this small boy sat very still, his eyes riveted to his primer, but his mind as free as the roving winds of autumn. It was a pesky nuisance to be so little, he thought. How he loathed his kilt suit and his primer! Those ABC's? Disgusting! "C-A-T"—while Charley Narimore and Llewellyn Dow were reading to Miss Bartow from McGuffy's Second Reader. And number work! Louis felt so smart that he could get up to a hundred. Who'd want to do that, anyhow?

A heavy frown sat upon the brow of this quasi-scholar. But wait—Miss Bartow was speaking to him. "Willard, wouldn't you like to count the windows and rafters and wheels and belts in the mill? And think how nice it would be to read what it says on the barrels of flour that your Grandfather is shipping way off somewhere. When you learn your numbers and your letters, you can do just that."

This was good work on the part of a young teacher whose training had not included child psychology. She had offered this beginner a target worth aiming at.

As a reward for a day of good conduct and earnest effort, Miss Bartow sometimes dismissed school early in order to visit the mill. Those were red-letter days for the Perkins boys. They swelled with pride to hear Miss Bartow declare the hum of the mill the best music in the world. Her interest in the mysterious process of turning wheat into flour was good to see.

The cooper shop was an exciting spot where men made barrels for Grandpa Perkins' flour. The head cooper explained that all barrel material came by barge from Charles May's stave factory in Excelsior. Mr. May's men cut great lengths of red and white oak into very thin layers, steaming those to be made pliable for staves. Lastly, they were cut into barrel lengths. Barrel heads were basswood disks, and the hoop poles were hickory saplings. Iron hoops had not yet come into use. Some folks made a fair living scouring the woods for hickory hoop poles.

To see a cooper assemble the material required for a barrel, and to watch him deftly slap it together with absolute precision was little short of magic in the eyes of small observers. Every cooper and every mill hand was pleased and proud to have "teacher" bring her school over, and none of the crew ever tired of answering questions. For their patience and kindness, "teacher" thanked them with the fine, sincere courtesy that proved contagious among her pupils.

The next day, Miss Bartow would have a lesson for the whole school on what they had learned at the mill and the cooper shop. That day, at least, little Willard was on a par with any of the big boys, because he knew all the answers.

As the weeks passed, school went better for Willard, but time often dragged. A thousand interesting things were waiting to be done after school. To go driving with the Narimore boys was the best fun of all. Charlie and Fred had broken in a couple of young oxen to drive with reins like horses, so that they both could get into the ox cart intead of having to walk beside the oxen and "gee-haw" them. Every time Miss Bartow was invited to take an ox drive, she went riding in state, sitting as gracefully upon the seat of that ox cart as a queen in her chariot.

Whenever Willie looked at his attractive young teacher, he was seized with a yearning tinged with rebellion against fate. There was no denying it, it was just plain tough to be nothing but a youngster. If he were only a few years older, Miss Bartow would surely marry him. They could live right in the mill. She wouldn't mind the dust; it was white anyway, like her apron. So little Willard dreamed on, beautiful gilt-edged dreams.

One day those dreams were torn to shreds. A little lad's rose-colored world fell in a heap of grey ashes because his Grandfather had sold the mill. With soul stripped bleak and barren, and with eyes blinded by tears, Willard bade good-bye to his mill, his ducks, his pigs, and his Miss Bartow. Tumbling into the lumber wagon piled with household goods, this young exponent of the first Minnetonka flour milling operation shut his eyes tight, put his hands to his ears to shut out the mill's sweet song, and rode away, not caring what might happen next.

NOTE: The Perkins families, upon leaving the Mills, settled on the section of land where the Hennepin County Fair is held and where the Hopkins High School now stands. Later Edward Perkins became a physician and settled his family in Excelsior. For many years, Dr. Perkins served much of this lake region as one of Dr. Hugh Arey's predecessors.

Part II — AS A BRIDE KNEW IT

The fatherless Dunham family looked forsaken and forlorn in spite of the pork pie steaming into their faces. Their absent sister was the topic of conversation at the moment.

"Why in thunder don't you tell her to come home, Ma? She's stayed a couple of weeks longer now than you said she could. I'm getting tired of trying to run this place without her."

Ma Dunham laughed in spite of herself. Her youngest son, the family storm center, sat frowning darkly into his plate while she went on cutting the pork pie into giant pieces for her five hungry boys. Fine fellows, but somehow they hadn't taken to pioneering worth a cent. Things had gone a little worse for the family every year, but there was nothing to do but to hang on.

Rain or shine, it was Mary who wove the gold into the fabric of each life under that family roof. With little sister still too young to be of much comfort, Ma Dunham could hardly imagine life without her cheery older girl. But here was Tom with the letter they'd been expecting from Mary for some time.

"Hurry, read it, Ma!" "When's she coming?" Mother Dunham scanned the letter rapidly. "Boys, there isn't a word about her coming home. Oh! wait, what's this? Good land, a whole sheet of figures, like print, and a little writing in a man's hand!"

Crowding around Ma's chair, the boys examined the page which was neat, attractive, businesslike, if not understandable. Then, as though by common consent, they began to read in chorus:

Mill, 78 x 58.................................4 stories high
Elevator, 30 x 40........30 feet high, storage 30,000 bu. wheat
Warehouse, 30 x 30 ....3 stories high

$$\text{Capacity} \begin{cases} 4,000 \text{ bbls. flour} \\ 50,000 \text{ bu. wheat} \\ 150 \text{ T. bran and shorts} \end{cases}$$

Cooper shop, 18 x 40..........................32 coopers
Mill equipment: 5 runs stone
                11 settes rolls
                11 purifiers
Output — 300 bbls. daily
Markets — New York City, Boston, points in Scandinavia, London, Paris.
Means of shipping — St. Paul and Manitoba R. R. running out from St. Paul to Wayzata. Survey is going on for new railroad nearer mill, the Minneapolis and St. Louis.
Present Minnetonka Mill Co., after several changes in ownership, is now headed by Loren Fletcher, Pres.; A. C. Loring, Treas.; and C. H. Burwell, Sec'y. Entire plant recently remodeled and modernized. Without doubt Minnetonka Milling has a bright future.

Ma folded up the sheet of figures and Mary's letter with deliberation. Why had Mary taken the trouble to send such definite information regarding the mill near her Uncle Ivory's place? She must have a reason behind all this.

"Well," Frank spoke with conviction, "Sis sure likes that flour mill."

"I don't blame her. At least it's a change from here!" put in Charley, the second son.

Ma jumped up from the table. "Boys, I've got an idea. Let's get some stakes, some yardsticks, and the square, and we'll lay out these buildings for ourselves right east of the barn."

Then came the fun. Activity is a first-class remedy for disappointment. In no time the boys forgot that Mary might not be home as soon as they had hoped; they forgot everything but the matter at hand. Just as Ma was crawling under the hayrack to drive a stake at the corner of the cooper shop, she heard a sweetly familiar voice: "Hello, Mama, what are you doing under there? And what are you boys up to, anyway? Aren't you one bit surprised to see me?" Mary put on a pretty pout.

The boys stood back, almost abashed before their sister, now taller and prettier than they had realized. Perhaps it was the new hat and the gracefully draped polonaise. But soon they crowded around her, showing her their newly laid-out mill site.

"Say, Sis, what doggone sucker wrote all this rubbish down for you? It's made us no end of trouble." Ed had spoken for all of them.

"His name is Charles Henry Burwell—and he isn't any sucker, I can tell you that!" Mary retorted. "What's more, he's going to be your brother-in-law in a couple of months if Mama says so."

*　　*　　*

Several weeks after Mary Dunham had gone home, the Minnetonka Mills sewing circle met to do some quilting. That day the conversation gradually drifted into speculation: was Charley Burwell pretty much in earnest about Mary Dunham, was he really serious?

"Well," declared Mrs. Works, "I'd say so, I'd say he'd 'bout made up his mind. You've all seen her picture he carries 'round in his Waterbury, haven't you?"

They had—all but one poor mortal who straightway threw her shawl over her head and hurried over to the mill office to inquire of Charley the time of day. Charley looked at his watch, and so did his visitor. Sure enough, there was Mary. Upon rejoining her sewing sisters, Mrs. Narimore proposed they start a quilt for the bride "right now"—and they did.

And so it came about that, when Mary returned to Minnetonka Mills as a bride, she was not coming into a strange place, although she *was* entering a new world; and the newness of Mary Burwell's world was not to be denied. Leaving behind a monotonously level prairie with its meadow larks and bobolinks, she had come to the varied ups and downs of a wooded lake district resounding with the lilting notes of wood thrushes and veeries. She had turned her back upon the silence of a solitary homestead and now stood facing the almost complete lack of privacy that results from the kindly sociability of a thriving little village. Without the least respect for mathematics, she had exchanged five large brothers, one small sister, and one middle-sized mother for *one* well-proportioned husband.

And the mill? Well, she hadn't exchanged anything for that; it had been thrown in for good measure. To this young woman, the mill and its adjacent buildings seemed like a somber jewel with an ever-changing setting. In spring, its background was infinite shadings of green followed by the pinks and creams of early summer blossoms. In autumn, this dark gem rested against the reds and yellows of fall foliage; in winter, it was hugged by the softly drifting snow. To this bride, just as to a small boy years before, the mill seemed like more than wood and stone.

Then there was the millpond, which furnished no end of diversion. In the summer Minnetonka Mills had the use of Mr. Burwell's small steamer, *Fresco,** which fumed and fussed around the millpond and then took to the lake with passengers and various kinds of freight. Whether steamers or barges or mere ducks skimmed its surface, whether its water mirrored the radiant sunset or simply froze stiff and silent—no matter, the millpond still was hers.

Welcomed by her husband's friends, she slipped into her place in community life and found it comfortable. She grew to regard

*Later the *Fresco,* under the name of *Why Not,* did lake service for many years.

neighborly espionage as friendly interest. She liked the mill hands and their families. They, in turn, "set store by her."

"How come that young Mis' Burwell's got sech a head fer figgers?" The foreman at the cooper shop scratched his head and tried to answer his own question. "Why, she kin tell the size o' every one o' these here buildin's and all about the mill machinery. And she was over yesterday inquirin' 'bout that new hundred-horsepower engine we're puttin' in. Plague take it, ef she didn't even know the name o' the thing. 'Reynolds Corliss,' sez she, glib's can be. How in time does she do it?"

Ma Dunham and the boys could have answered the foreman's question. They hadn't laid out the Minnetonka Mill site back of their barn for nothing, nor had they played the "mill game" without results after Mary's return home. At mealtime somebody would say "cooper shop" or "warehouse," and they'd each try to be first with correct dimensions. Lots of fun! They had played that game until Mary left on her wedding day, so of course this bride had a "head for figgers."

From her kitchen window, Mary could see the grain being brought to the mill. Barges piled high with wheat streamed down Minnehaha Creek from the lake, while mile-long processions of ox carts brought grain by land. Excelsior served as a shipping point for farmers coming from as far west as Lac Qui Parle County. They headed straight for Excelsior, dumped their wheat on the waiting barges, then lived on crackers and cheese in W. B. Jones' grocery store till their flour and shorts returned next day via the same barges.

Business was thriving but, in any business, difficulties arise. One morning Charles Burwell hurried back home much perplexed. His bride was doing the breakfast dishes as he entered.

"Mary," he said, "something has happened. Eight German farmers have already come with their loads, and every mother's son of them has brought back the flour he took home the last time. They say our flour is a failure, that 'twon't make bread fit for a hog! They're plenty loud-mouthed about it, too. Looks like they're trying to spoil our business. They demand 'decent' flour in exchange for what they brought back. I've put all their returned sacks to the left of the warehouse door—inside. To the right are dozens of new sacks of flour ground yesterday.

"Now, can't you go down and bring back a pint or so out of some of those new sacks to the right of the door. Mark each sack, and then maybe you could bake a little sample loaf for each of these fellows. Do you think they could come back around five o'clock, so they could have their loaf for supper? The sacks to the *right*, remember!"

Whatever Mary Burwell's answer was, it seemed to satisfy her husband. A little later she stood in the warehouse, pail and pint cup in hand. Making sure she was alone, she measured out a pint of flour from each of the returned sacks, on the left.

At five o'clock eight big Germans were filling Mary's kitchen with loud exclamations of delight over the fresh bread. "*Ach Himmel!*" "*Mein Gott!*" "*Wundervoll!*" "*Gut genug für die Engel!*" Mary assured each one that he should have the exact sack from which his loaf was made.

Supper was not ready when Mary's husband came an hour later. She explained the delay and asked him to go down with her to the warehouse to make sure of the right sacks for the Germans next day.

"What's the use? You marked them, didn't you?"

"Please come," and Mary started off. Her husband was hungry; he was glum (such whims as women have!), but he followed.

"Here are the sacks"—she was pointing to the forlorn, rejected bunch of returns.

"What, not these! How could you have made such a mistake? Didn't I say the sacks on the right?"

Mary laughed. "These 'failures' made the dandiest bread those Germans ever saw, Charles. Really prize-winning bread. Come, let's tie 'em up with new string, brush 'em off nice and clean, and pull 'em over into a new place—and they'll be ready to go back the same way they came."

Charles Burwell gave his wife an odd look. "You'll do!" he said approvingly.

The next day eight happy men each carried back their kitchen-tested flour, the flour that had made the best bread they'd ever thrown over lip. Now Gretchen's bread would be like Mrs. Burwell's—"*Gott sei Dank.*" Behind the kitchen curtains stood that young lady watching their departure with genuine pleasure. "What they don't know won't hurt them," she said with a smile.

The hum of the mill might have spelled monotony for some women, but not for Mary. To her it was welcome music. It meant business. Business took a step forward when strong, fast-stepping horses replaced oxen. Horses brought bigger loads, but they made more muss for a certain neat housewife. To the teamsters, the Burwell porch seemed the ideal place to hitch horses—handy at noon and night to dump oats and ground feed right out on the porch floor! After the horses had devoured their feed, they went right on nibbling at the porch.

"Business is business," so not a word of complaint came from within. As soon as the horses left, however, a young housewife, armed with hammer and sturdy ten-penny spikes, set to work. When she was done, the ends of the porch boards presented an even row of nail heads. The nails, driven lengthwise into every porch board, would be a surprise to the next relay of horses.

By 1879, the Minnetonka Milling Company had come into its own. A long-distance telephone line, the first in the state and second in the United States according to George Burwell, the son, was extended from Minneapolis to Minnetonka Mills for commercial purposes only. This line had to use No. 9 iron wire which brought to the proprietors of Minnetonka Mills in their Minneapolis office the hum of bees, the barking of dogs, and the croaking of bullfrogs in the millpond nearby.

The mill, once a custom gristmill, had ceased to be such and now purchased the wheat outright. Paper money, since Civil War times, had lost value to such an extent that people clamored for gold. Since Minnetonka Milling Company paid in gold, its business grew by leaps and bounds.

One day the company faced a crisis. Long processions of teams were waiting to unload. The men from great distances expected immediate cash, but the safe was empty. Mr. Burwell could not leave, nor could anyone else connected with the mill—except Mary Burwell.

Without a word, as unconcernedly as you please, Mrs. Burwell saddled her horse, put on her long riding habit, adjusted her broad-brimmed hat with its flowing veil, drew on her neatly fitting gloves, tickled her mount with her smart riding whip and was off to Minneapolis, presumably to spend the day with a friend. But no, not that day! Instead, she went to the bank, drew out $5,000 in gold, slipped the bulky package into a bag under her sidesaddle, and started for home. Under a brave exterior, a timid heart beat in double-quick time every inch of the ten miles back, through wooded country, to Minnetonka Mills; but she made it!

* * *

Upon her first visit to Minnetonka Mills, Mary Dunham was grieved that St. John's Episcopal Chapel was being used for school purposes. She learned that a pioneer missionary, the Rev. J. S. Chamberlain, had built this chapel in 1858, the first church in all the Minnetonka region. When Mary came to the settlement later as a bride, this tiny chapel lay heavy upon her heart. Why not build a modest schoolhouse and thus release the little church for divine worship? Gradually the young woman stirred up the interest of her neighbors and also the enthusiasm of Mr. Fletcher and Mr. Loring, owners of the mill. At last, a small school building was erected.

After the chapel was repaired came the day of reconsecration. That ceremony brought Minnesota's great Bishop Whipple, a man who understood the human heart whether it beat in a white man's or a red man's breast. From that day, the good bishop felt a personal interest in the welfare of the little chapel. The whole settlement, as well as the Burwell family, found in this great man a benign and blessed friend.

Some time later, the Reverend Mr. Graves served the St. John's parish. Once upon a Sunday, when the mill was running full force, he drove in unexpectedly. Mr. Burwell, feeling a sense of guilt for the whole company, explained that the big crops and late season made this Sunday work necessary. The clergy-man was quick to see the troubled look on his parishioner's face. "Don't worry, my son," he said, "I know just how it is. In fact, I can forget all about it if I find a few sacks of flour under my buggy seat, for my poor people."

Mary Burwell was an ardent church worker, a good business woman, and a real home body. As a bride, she had come to live in a house, once a hotel built by Mr. Perkins, standing at the right of Minnetonka Boulevard as one faces Minneapolis. With real regret she left this first home for a new one across the millpond. Her new house, lifting its cupola high in the trees, commanded a perfect view of the millpond and the mill which stood opposite the present Burwell school. (This school, by the way, represents one of Mary Burwell's later interests. It stands on the site presented to the district by Mrs. Burwell herself.)

A cozy little family, a new home, many friends, a little church, a schoolhouse, a mill, a millpond and a steamboat: her life at Minnetonka Mills held for Mary Burwell a large measure of idyllic happiness. For all these blessings, Mrs. Burwell offered up humble and devout thanks every Sabbath day in the tiny chapel nearby.

Then a change came. The Minnetonka Milling Company sold the mill property to a couple of Canadians. The mill was closed in honor of the transaction. When there seemed to be no intention of reopening the mill, Charles Burwell bought the entire mill property, planning to run the mill as usual.

Fate interfered at this point. According to the Burwells' daughter Louise, all sorts of untoward circumstances militated against reopening business. The Washburn-Crosby and the Pillsbury Mills were daily improving and enlarging their output. This meant tremendous competition. Besides, for several successive years, grasshoppers had been on the increase.

"As far as the grasshoppers are concerned," continued Louise Burwell in conversation with friends, "billions of them came in black clouds from the Dakota border. They bent the wheat stalks to the ground with their weight and made enough noise eating to be heard a mile away. After staying a few days, they deposited millions of eggs and then disappeared. I've heard my father tell how Governor Pillsbury set aside a day of prayer, April 26, 1877. Only a deep freeze could destroy those eggs, and it was too late in the spring for such a thing to happen, but everybody prayed all that day anyway. Guess the State never had so much praying done, before or since."

"And what happened?" someone asked. Miss Burwell stepped to the bookcase, opened an old book, turned a few pages, and then looked pleased. "Governor Pillsbury's own words give the answer," she said. "Here they are: 'And the very next night it turned cold and froze every grasshopper in the State stiff; froze 'em right up solid, sir. Well, that was over twenty years ago, and the grasshoppers don't seem to have been bothering us much since.'

"So much for the grasshoppers," said Louise Burwell, "but the chinch bugs followed the grasshoppers, and they continued for many years to damage the wheat crop in all parts of the State."

Added to these misfortunes was the fact that shore dwellers along Lake Minnetonka began to object to the lowering of the water line for industrial purposes. Some even hinted at court action; others proposed building a dam at Gray's Bay in order to stabilize the water level. So it came about that for years the mill stood sad and silent. Finally, shorn of its equipment, it was wrecked, in 1900, for its lumber which was later used in the construction of a Minneapolis flour mill. And that was the end of Minnetonka milling.

Life is full of strange contradictions. Once upon a time a little boy, blinded with tears, had had to leave his mill. Upon a bride his mantle of affection for that mill had fallen. To her its music, its bustle, the very romance of its existence became a matter of personal pride. And then—the *mill* had had to leave the bride.

Both partings brought grief, but there was a difference. To part with an object of deep affection in childhood brings an agony unspeakable and unforgettable. A similar experience in adult years should be met with the philosophy of resignation. Change is certain to come, and one should meet it with courage.

Just how Mrs. Burwell felt while the mill was standing there, neglected and forlorn, or what went on inside her soul when the wrecking crew began to tear down what had been the center of life when she came as a bride in '76, no one ever knew. St. John's Chapel had also disappeared, leaving another vacancy in life as she had known it.

Still another loss was headed her way. Her millpond began to shrink when the dam at Gray's Bay became a reality in 1897. From the moment she arrived as a bride, Mary Burwell had taken delight in her millpond. Now the day had come for filling it in and planting the trees which today shade and shelter the fine old Burwell residence.

"You see," she used to say, "we really have a much larger lawn now that the millpond is gone."

CHAPTER XIII

Minnetonka's
Sea Dog

OVER twenty years ago, if you had happened to be on the streets of Excelsior, Mound, or Wayzata, you might have caught sight of "Cap" Johnson, Minnetonka's sea dog. He belonged to all the lake. He belonged to everybody. He had a way of remembering people and of being remembered himself, judging from this incident cited in the *Northwest Tourist*.

It seems that while cruising the Mediterranean, a Londoner and a Philadelphia woman had fallen into earnest conversation. They had struck common ground—both had visited Lake Minnetonka in the 80's.

"And you knew that jolly tar, 'Cap' Johnson, didn't you?" the Englishman asked.

"Oh, yes! Positively huge, wasn't he?"

"I say now, those moonlight dances, remember?" Yes, she'd had the time of her life at one of them!

"Well," continued the Englishman, "one night when nobody had planned a dance, the *City of St. Louis* called for guests, anyway. The evening started out quiet enough: a spell over everything; water like glass; mists along shore; trees still as ghosts; thick silence, thick enough to slice with a sword—and then suddenly, the wild cry of a loon or the crazy laugh of a screech owl. Eerie, positively weird, don't you know.

"When the silence got oppressive, somebody asked 'Cap' Johnson to sing—and could he sing? Voice as clear as a bell, powerful, too; other times tender and sweet as a woman's. One Norwegian folk song, he explained to us first, told how the old women were trying to find a wife for a confirmed bachelor.

'Cap' acted it all out as he sang it. 'Pon my word, 'twas a side-splitter; never saw anything in vaudeville to equal it.

"After we'd settled down a bit, 'Cap' began singing hymns, and we joined in when we knew the words. Then he began repeating Psalms, maybe a dozen or so, and, by Jove, he meant every bloomin' word of them. Never have felt so religious before or since."

The Englishman had spoken with real feeling. His companion met his mood by suggesting that maybe 'Cap' was still singing back there on Lake Minnetonka. As a matter of fact, he was, and he kept right on singing the rest of his life. When somebody asked him why, he replied it was because he had come here to Minnetonka. This is how it happened.

One spring day in 1881, a strapping young man strode back and forth in front of a Minneapolis railway station, waiting for a Duluth-bound train. After a few weeks' visit with his sister, he still had his sea legs. When a lad has sailed every sea of the globe for eight years, he grows sea legs that stay with him for life.

That visit in his sister's home had done something to this young man, just come of age. An uncomfortable nostalgia tugged at his heart. Home! His home back in Norway. What fun he and his brothers and sisters used to have when they lived in Kristian Sand. His sister had reminded him of many things he'd forgotten: how they used to wave and whistle at the northern lights shooting bright-colored streamers across the sky of black velvet; and how as soon as spring came they ran up into the mountains to find the first flowers for mother.

Home! No, he was not bound for home; it was Australia this time. Could such a roving sailor ever have a home, his own home? That was a new thought. His *own* home, he liked the sound of it. There was Mina now—he had met her at his sister's. *There* was a real girl, mighty fine, mighty nice—and did anybody ever see anything as cute as those curls behind her ears? When a young man thinks such thoughts, he has left this world behind and has entered one of his own.

"What's your name, young man?"

"John R. Johnson," came the prompt reply of this sailor-trained lad. In front of the startled young Norseman, just returning from his dream world, stood a fashionably dressed man with silk hat, gloves, and cane—a man who gazed at him with a look of open admiration. Was it his size or his sea legs that attracted the Hon. W. D. Washburn? Well, no matter.

By way of introduction, General Washburn explained to the young man what his business interests were: Minneapolis flour milling and railroading. He was, in fact, the president of the Minneapolis and St. Louis road. Then, with enthusiasm, Mr. Washburn launched into the story of his pet project. At Wayzata he was having the finest steamboat built that this part of the country had ever seen. He planned to run this steamer in connection with his railroad. Lake Minnetonka, he felt confident, was rapidly rising in popularity. His new boat would mean big business. Would young Johnson like a job on his new steamer?

Not quite sure that all this beautiful story could be true, John R. Johnson acted with unusual sagacity. He showed hesitancy, definite reluctance. Just where was Minnetonka? How did one get there? Could a person have a little time to consider such an offer? Mr. Washburn seemed not at all displeased at the young man's apparent reluctance and suggested that he take a look at the lake for himself.

Soon the well-dressed businessman and the young sailor were on their way to Minnetonka in the Washburn carriage behind a handsome span of horses driven by a colored coachman. At the lake, there was Mr. Washburn's steamboat being built just as he had said. The young Norwegian accepted the job offered him. When the *City of St. Louis* was launched July 9, 1881, John R. Johnson went aboard as first mate, to become captain of this floating palace the following year. Then it was that Captain Johnson turned thought into action—there was Mina, you know.

In the fall of '82, they were married. A wife, a home, a steamboat, a lake—could a young man ask for more? John Johnson felt that that was enough. He couldn't help singing and repeating poetry—Longfellow, Whittier, or Wordsworth—to give expression to his inner joy. Life was good here on Minnetonka.

Minnetonka Story

Only once in his seventeen years of service on the *City of St. Louis* did Captain Johnson come face to face with tragedy. One day a sudden squall ripped across the lake. There was no danger to his stately steamer, but the captain on the upper deck had a seaman's eye. He saw a white sail give a quick dip and then disappear.

Calling the nearest deck hand, he bade him lower the lifeboat. In an instant, both captain and deck hand were far out, heading for the point of disaster. Reaching the spot where the sailboat had capsized, "Cap" threw off his clothes and began to dive in search of the drowning victims.

Success came at last. One after the other, he loaded the four half-drowned men into the lifeboat. Like mad, the captain and deck hand pulled for the *City*. While still afar off, "Cap," in that big voice of his, commanded the stewards to stand ready with hot blankets and restoratives. In due time, E. S. Parson and his three St. Louis friends were as good as new, in spite of their close call. Captain Johnson, too, was none the worse for the wear—better, in fact, by a handsome gold watch presented to him later, with a medal bearing the names of the four persons rescued and a cut of their sailboat.

* * *

It is next to impossible to give the modern sophisticate a fair idea of the grandeur of hotel and boat service during Minnetonka's halcyon years. Judged by today's standards, it doesn't seem extraordinary, but for that scantily equipped and poorly lighted generation, Minnetonka spelled splendor.

When the *City* steamed out into Wayzata Bay for the first time, people held their breath at the "sweet" running of her St. Louis-made engines. Never had they seen anything like her easy speed. The real surprise came, however, when Captain Johnson snapped on the electric lights. Passengers gazed speechless at the blazing chandeliers. To be sure, the large hotels, such as the Lafayette and St. Louis, were lighted with both gas and electricity, but at home, the kerosene lamp was still in vogue.

Even in Minneapolis, illumination by electricity was to remain, for years to come, an unfulfilled hope. For a steamboat to be lighted electrically was, therefore, almost unbelievable. No other inland boat in the United States at that time was lighted in this fashion. At night the *City of St. Louis* gleamed and sparkled like a cluster of diamonds.

Once when school children asked "Cap" Johnson how long the *City* was, he told them to take a yardstick and lay it down, end on end, fifty-four times for its length and fourteen times for its width. He loved to tell how handsome a boat she was—pure white, her black smokestacks edged with red—graceful she was as any swan.

If possible had "nerves" back in the 80's, a ride on the *City* must have proved a soothing remedy. One could rock back and forth in comfortable easy chairs in the mahogany-finished cabin while resting one's feet on thick-napped Smyrnas. There were silk flags of all nations on every hand, and a forest of plate-glass mirrors on all sides.

Captain Johnson rejoiced over every detail of his beautiful boat's equipment—especially the dining room with its lovely linens, the silverware marked "City of St. Louis," the delicate China, the cut flowers, the well-trained band, the Indian dancers, and the clowns. Best of all were the five hundred guests that could be efficiently served at one sitting at "a dollar per." All this splendor contrasted very favorably with the drab dangers attending the seafaring life he had once known.

From the day of her launching in '81, the *City of St. Louis* was all the rage. Season after season she was crowded to capacity. She was not the biggest boat on the lake, but she had the biggest captain, big of body and mind.

Struggle with storms at sea had given Captain Johnson unusual physical prowess. Winds and waves had done more than develop his physical strength; they had washed and scoured his soul clean of the little meannesses and prejudices that sometimes clutter up the thinking of landlubbers.

Captain Johnson loved life. He loved people; they interested him, puzzled him, entertained him. When the passengers talked with him, he expressed views so cosmopolitan that they recognized him as a citizen of the world.

Those were happy days for the captain. He loved his little inland sea and his beautiful boat. In fact, he was glad when insurance requirements made it necessary to live several winters on his boat, anchored at Solberg's Point. A perfect home it made for his family; moreover, two of his daughters, Mrs. Hehl and Mrs. Mase, were born on board the *City of St. Louis.*

At the peak of Minnetonka's popularity, there existed among all the steamers, for a time, a good-natured rivalry for patronage. Later, competition lost its playfulness and grew grim and dangerous. One day while speeding into the Wayzata harbor, the *Belle of Minnetonka* crowded the *City of St. Louis* out of its regular course. Captain Johnson shouted orders to his pilot, who failed to obey. Disaster seemed inevitable. Like a thunderbolt, "Cap" Johnson crashed down into the engine room from somewhere on upper deck. Seizing the controls, he jerked the engines into reverse himself. Not a second too soon and only by inches, the beautiful *City* was saved from smashing her prow upon the pier.

On that occasion Captain Johnson's Viking temper was brought out for a good airing. First of all, his own pilot was given attention. Old Thor, the god of thunder, could not have done a more finished job. Next the captain of the *Belle of Minnetonka,* "that cattle boat," got all that was coming to him. Extreme carelessness, trickery, or any sort of injustice called forth such fire and brimstone from that big man that one wondered if he could ever return to his usual jovial good nature. But the storm was soon over, and "Cap" Johnson was himself again.

In an effort to eliminate rivalry, the Lake Minnetonka Navigation Company (L.M.N. Co.) gathered all the other lake steamers, including the *Belle of Minnetonka,* under one management. Then the *City of St. Louis,* competing with a whole fleet, added many new attractive features for entertainment during meals and through the evening hours. No use! Finally, when W. D. Washburn was offered a fancy price for his *City,* he accepted it.

Captain Johnson was implored to superintend the whole fleet

and consented to do so. Competition came to an end, but something else was coming to an end also. Minnetonka's popularity had started downgrade. In a few years, the L.M.N. Co. offered Captain Johnson the entire fleet and the landings at Excelsior and Solberg's Point for only $3,000. The bottom had dropped out of the steamboat business.

During the next ten years, Captain Johnson proved that he had horse sense as well as sailor sense. He accepted the change with keen interest in his new setup. Smaller boats were his answer to a shrinking transportation project. Consequently, he repaired and remodelled the smaller boats while building new, modish ones (the *Plymouth*, the *Mayflower*, the *Puritan*, and others) to compete with rival steamboats: the *Mabel Lane*, Smithtown Bay; the *Florence M. Deering*, Crystal Bay and West Arm; the *Comet*, Maxwell and Stubbs Bays; and the *Kenosha*, later Capt. George Hopkins' *Victor*.

The *Belle of Minnetonka* had already been run up into St. Albans Bay to rust away out of sight. The little Johnson girls played hide-and-seek among her stanchions and often found birds' nests in the openings of her capstan, so quickly do time and disuse claim things abandoned. The bell, once the pride of Minnetonka's biggest steamer, was rescued from a junk pile by Herbert Morse and a group of Excelsior citizens and hung in Excelsior's grade-school building where it rings to this day.

During the period of small steamboats, Captain Johnson enjoyed one huge triumph. From Oslo, in 1905, came a male chorus of over a hundred voices. Their concerts in Minneapolis and St. Paul were highlights in the world of music. Captain Johnson missed not a single concert and, when their season was over, he entertained the whole group at a banquet aboard the *Puritan* and took them around the lake by moonlight. When the chorus began to sing the old folk songs, a new voice, rich and full of feeling, swelled the volume of song. With these Norsemen, Captain Johnson sang himself back to his fatherland.

In the year 1906, a new era dawned for this lake region. That year separate streetcar lines nosed their way beyond Excelsior, and into Deephaven also. The streetcar company bought Captain Johnson's fleet and changed many of his steamers into streetcar boats called "yellow jackets."

At this point John R. Johnson created a new job for himself. For years he had had an idea that some parts of Lake Minnetonka should be dredged. Now here was a chance to put that idea to work. He salvaged old unused boats by making them into tugs—his beloved *City of St. Louis*, for example, furnished material for two tugs. "After all," he remarked to a friend, "the *City* would rather wear out than rust out, I'm pretty sure."

Purchasing a dredging machine, "Cap" entered upon a new career, the dredging business. Since he did not need to spend all his time upon the lake in this enterprise, he began to adapt himself to land residence. Without complaint or regret, he met the changes as though they were actually to his advantage.

He began with renewed interest to support church and lodge and school. The Congregational Church in Excelsior received as a gift from him the pulpit mural, "Christ in the Garden." School athletics he espoused with an enthusiasm good to see. Once when Excelsior's basketball team missed, by a hair's breadth, the championship trip to Chicago, Captain Johnson took the team himself and enjoyed the trip the best of any of the boys.

And so life went on for Captain Johnson, until one spring day in 1931. That day the streets of Excelsior were silent. People spoke softly and moved about quietly. Just fifty years after coming to the lake he loved so well, Minnetonka's sea dog had booked passage for HOME.

CHAPTER XIV | *Sailing on*
Minnetonka

IT SEEMED unendurably hot on that Louisiana bus full of GI's until the word "lake" came to my ears, bringing with it a breath of cool air.

"Yup, I've tried everything but Granddad's lake. The Atlantic, Lake Michigan, even good old Mississippi."

A young lieutenant and his buddy were talking about sailing, probably trying to forget the heat in the crowded bus headed for camp not far from New Orleans. The young officer's pal yawned and asked, "Your Granddad's lake, Jim? What about it?"

"Oh, nothing much," was the reply, "except there's where I'm going the minute this infernal war is over. Think I'd like to do some honest-to-gosh sailing, for once!"

After a moment's silence, the lieutenant added, "You know, there's a family living somewhere around that lake that I'm going to look up, name of Bert—Bert—h'm, that's not just it, something like that though. Anyhow, I'm looking 'em up. Great skippers, according to Granddad. They knew their stuff, those Berts."

Now discretion may be the better part of valor, but curiosity sometimes gets one further, so I leaned across the aisle and asked, "Do you, by any chance, mean Burton?"

"That's it, Burton's the name," he exclaimed, "but how do you happen to know?"

By way of answer I handed him my purse-size map of Minnetonka. "For gosh sakes," he exclaimed, "Lake Minnetonka, sure's thunder! Of all the times Granddad's told me about sailing her, I'd never seen a map of her. Look at all those darn bays. Bet the wind plays hide-and-seek 'round there in great shape—plenty of squalls, too."

His excited enthusiasm roused the other passengers who crowded around to hear how Granddad had sailed on that lake in the 90's. Now that Lt. Jim has licked the Nazis and the Japs, Minnetonka yachtsmen may some day find a difficult rival in that service man whose grandfather regarded this lake as a sailor's Mecca. We hope by the time Lt. Jim arrives the lake will still be high enough to spill over Gray's Bay dam.

If, however, another dry cycle should occur, seven county pumps could go into action. They are silent now, but ready to forestall another all-time low of eighty inches below the top of Gray's Bay dam. That "low" of 1937 was a distressing experience. We realized then that without the lake, this locality would become a desolate spot, no matter how lovely summer days might be.

Around this lake not only days in June are rare, but perfect days come all summer long. One such August day some twenty-five years ago our family found itself aboard the *Victor*, waiting for the annual yacht race to start from the Minnetonka Yacht Club House.

Everybody was happy with eager anticipation. Suddenly a pistol shot announced the race was on. A beautiful sight were those white sails outlined against the blue sky, gliding in silent majesty across the sky-blue water.

But those sailboats held no charm whatever for one passenger aboard the *Victor*. An old lady from Nebraska sat motionless, gazing down at the water as though hypnotized. Finally words came. "Land sakes," she exclaimed with a sweeping gesture, "look at all this water would you? Never saw so much in one place in all my born days! Folks at home jes' won't believe it no matter how emphatic I tell 'em."

When someone asked her how she was enjoying the race, the expression that came over her face was something to remember. "Race?" she said. "You sure ain't callin' *that* a race! Why, a race is where somebody does somethin'. Land sakes, all them sailors air a-doin' is jes' a-settin' still and a-lettin' the wind blow 'em along."

To appreciate the fine points of a yacht race, one must now and then give his whole attention to the matter at hand; but an occasional lull in the excitement is the time to listen to the tales of one's steamboat captain.

Captain George Hopkins gave us a look of compassion that day when we told him this was our first yacht race. "Too bad," his voice was sorrowful, "we've been havin' 'em since '82. Sailboats came in long before the big boats and big hotels went. They sort of tied up the good old days to these times. But sailboats are goin' to stay."

Captain Hopkins was right. Sailboats are going to stay. And why? Simply because sailing never fails to offer a challenge, to demand a high degree of skill. In short, sailing is a fine art, and art is imperishable.

In 1882, exactly thirty years after the red man was invited to lift his canoe out of this lake and move on, there appeared upon Minnetonka a fleet of fifteen sailboats. The debut of that white-winged squadron created a stir of surprised excitement among summer visitors.

Those early yachtsmen sailed for the sheer fun of the thing. Westbrook Pegler's father, then living in Excelsior, once remarked: "Those first yachtsmen sailed with the most utter abandon and with completely reckless pleasure. The 'good sailors' were those who could carry the most sail without capsizing. Skippers carried rock or sand ballast which could be manipulated skillfully enough to keep the boat from turning turtle."

Although this was great sport, such playing around was slow to develop actual yachting skill. But when three genuine "salts" threw their hats into the ring, things began to happen. The records speak of these three as the "fathers of Minnetonka yachting": William Peet, son of the founder of the Atlantic Yacht Club; Hazen Burton, accustomed to salt-water yachting in Boston Bay; and H. C. McLeod of Halifax, a sailor and designer of boats.

The Minnetonka Yacht Club was organized in '87 and grew

like a mushroom, absorbing the members of the earlier, loosely organized Excelsior Yacht Club. The oldest club records list the names of these early sailors: Ward C. Burton, Alfred F. Pillsbury, Hazen J. Burton, William Peet, H. C. McLeod, Fred Hardenbergh, George V. Doerr, Harlow and Edward Gale, Charles and William Bovey, E. J. Phelps, and C. B. Eustis.

By 1889, the members decided to erect a clubhouse on a small island in St. Louis Bay. A year later the home of the Minnetonka Yacht Club, built by Harry W. Jones, was ready for use. J. M. Cowles, a correspondent for the *Northwest Tourist*, felt that this clubhouse was a "happy piece of architecture," molded into the picture so artfully that it seemed to be a natural part of its beautiful setting.

While skippers were learning the art of sailing on Lake Minnetonka, there was, in Bristol, Rhode Island, a certain blind man who later entered Minnetonka's yachting picture. John Herreshoff, in spite of his blindness, kept on designing new and startling types of sailing craft. New York and Boston newspapers spread far and wide the fame of Herreshoff's miraculous boats.

In British waters, Herreshoff's models repeatedly swept ahead of English and Scotch sailboats, until at last Sir Thomas Lipton, the best skipper in the British Isles, declared it was useless to compete with Herreshoff. In Lipton's own words: "That amazing American, adhering to the given water line, manages to produce year after year, vessels of greater and greater sail spread with hulls of more and more power."

This and more found a place in the conversation of the yachtsmen of Midwestern lakes. Enthusiasm for sailing grew daily. Yacht clubs were formed in Minnesota, Illinois, and Wisconsin. To these clubs Bostonians and New Yorkers shipped their cast-off sailboats, then straightway bought the Herreshoff models.

Even with those second-hand boats Midwestern yachting circles found sloops (two sail) and cat boats (one sail)—both of shallow draught—best adapted to lake sailing. These fresh-water skippers realized that finer skill in sailing made sand bags unnecessary; consequently, they ruled out such ballast by the end of the 80's.

For every yachtsman in the Middle West the name of Herreshoff possessed a charm of its own. Minnetonka skippers began to sigh by day and to dream by night of a Herreshoff on this lake. One day E. J. Phelps returned from the East with the lovely *Alpha*, a Herreshoff centerboard craft of beautiful form and alarming speed. Straightway Messrs. Peet and Dunwoody sent East for the *Kite*, of Herreshoff make.

Two famous models on our lake might not have been too many, but when Hazen Burton heard that a third Herreshoff, the *Coquina*, was on the way here, that was too much. He and his son Ward put the matter up to young Arthur Dyer, who admitted he had always "tinkered at designing sailboat models." The result was the canoe-like *Onawa*, which slipped *over* rather than *through* the water and glided by everything else afloat with such speed and grace that it was pronounced the eighth wonder of the world. The season of '93 was a continual triumph for the *Onawa* and its skipper, Ward Burton, a young sailor of consummate skill.

The Herreshoff models had at last been eclipsed. The yachting world went into mourning: a western boat builder had cast down their idol. New York and Boston commented fully on Minnetonka yachting, playing up the Burtons' find—Arthur Dyer. Other boat builders (Andrew Peterson of Excelsior, R. C. Moore of Wayzata, and Gus Amundson of White Bear) gained courage from Mr. Dyer's success and came forward with their designs for sailing craft.

At the close of the 80's, St. Paul formed a club on White Bear Lake. Some of its skippers manifested such skill in sailing that their club suggested to the Minnetonka Yacht Club a series of three inter-lake regattas to take place on these terms: the first regatta should be held at White Bear in '95; the second should occur on Lake Minnetonka in '96; while the final one, in '97, should come off on White Bear Lake. Furthermore, the club winning two of the three contests should be proclaimed the champion of the season, and the club winning two out of three seasons should win the silver cup in each class and the championship of both lakes.

Minnetonka Story

Minnetonka yachtsmen received the idea with enthusiasm. Feeling that White Bear's yachts were strictly inferior and St. Paul yachtsmen a trifle green at the sailing business, one Minnetonka skipper voiced the sentiments of his club when he expressed himself thus: "Well, if those White Bear folks really want to make us a present of a couple of silver cups, why all right, we will help them carry out their laudable desire. In fact, we'll take all the trophies they offer us."

Minnetonka's sailboats were put in perfect condition for that first regatta of '95. They were loaded onto wagons and taken by team to White Bear Lake a day early.

The next morning, high-stepping horses and shiny carriages fell into the procession. Minnetonka and Minneapolis were going visiting; White Bear and St. Paul were expecting them. White Bear homes threw open their doors to guests. Lawns were hung with hammocks and bristled with easy chairs. Seeing these preparations, Minnetonkans had an uncomfortable thought—it was going to be most embarrassing to win *all* the events away from such lavish hosts.

They say that the events of that '95 regatta were thrilling to behold. The weather was perfect. The skippers on both sides were keyed to a high pitch of excellence. Excitement grew beyond bounds as White Bear won event after event. Just why Dame Fortune turned her back on Minnetonka yachtsmen that day is still an unanswered question, but she did. She sat tight and grim, passing out all the plums with a smile to the White Bear skippers. Final results showed White Bear the winner of every event.

Hope was not dead; merely stunned. Were there not two more regattas ahead? There was opportunity yet to win the championship of both lakes, and that was precisely what Minnetonka yachtsmen determined to do.

The '96 regatta was scheduled for our lake. Enormous plans were made for the entertainment of the thousands who came from Wisconsin and Illinois, from Boston and New York to see Minnetonka win.

Again, as the regatta began, it was evident that Madame Fortune was still in an ugly mood. She gave Minnetonka not a single smile until the *Tartar* (built by Andrew Peterson, of Excelsior) swept past the Herreshoff model *Alfrida*. This was Minnetonka's happiest moment. In this second regatta the two yacht clubs tied for honors, and Minnetonka received her share of cups and pennants.

For the '97 regatta to be held at White Bear, even more elaborate plans than before were put into action. Minnetonka yachtsmen went at this last contest with new hope. They entered event after event with untiring pluck but, when the last race ended, they had not a single score to their credit. Hope was gone; Minnetonka had struck bottom. Cups and pennants won in the second regatta were handed over to victorious White Bear. Our skippers came home with plenty of nothing.

During the fifty years following those regattas with White Bear, sailing on Minnetonka has gained in popularity. Recently the Deephaven *Argus* expressed this word of appreciation with reference to Minnetonka yachting: "There is nothing more delightful than white sails against azure sky and black waters. Blown by the will of the wind, like big white birds, they move with grace across the great expanse of lake. For all lovers of dashing spray and whipping wind, an exciting and thrilling time is in store whenever yachts go a-racing."

| CHAPTER XV | *Minnetonka's* |
| | *Boat Builder* |

THERE used to live on the shore of Carson's Bay a man who once climbed to fame and took the lake along with him. This man was Arthur Dyer.

Fame has been defined as the lofty reputation derived from great achievements. The world has always considered such "lofty reputation" something greatly to be desired and difficult of attainment; yet, in its July 28, 1895, issue, the Minneapolis *Times* confidently coupled this coveted word fame with the name of our friend and neighbor, as follows:

"Mr. Dyer's fame and with it the renown of Minnetonka (of which we are justly proud) has extended beyond this grand old commonwealth of Minnesota, beyond the boundaries of Canada, beyond the confines of Buzzard's Bay and New York Harbor, beyond the surf-beaten coast of the Atlantic seaboard, beyond the sea itself even to the far distant boundaries of China."

If fame rests upon notable achievements, when, how, and what did Mr. Dyer achieve? The easiest way to find the answer was to ask the gentleman himself. This was his reply:

"Father ran a boat shop in Excelsior from 1879 to the middle of the 90's. As a youngster, I worked around the shop making models and toy sailboats.

"I got the idea that a saucer-like boat would skim over the water. It would lift the bow up instead of driving through the water. I made a model with a long slender bow. The yachtsmen around the boathouse called it a Dutch boat because the bow was cut away. I was twelve years old at this time.

"Up to this period, the racing boats were built to carry large sail area. The boats were very wide, usually half as wide as they were long. A few were narrow and deep, built to carry ballast and in this way give power.

"My idea of a narrow shallow boat of low power looked good to some, but no one would put up the money for the experiment. I went West to the Pacific coast when I was sixteen. In 1889, I returned and worked at boat building with my Father, Captain Sawin H. Dyer."

Analyze this account of the childhood and youth of a boat builder in embryo. "As a youngster . . . making models and toy sailboats." Note the gradual development—at first, work with the hands and then, the work of an active, growing mind. Result: "I got the idea." Behind all invention and discovery, behind all progress, there has always been "the idea."

Young Dyer held on to his idea, even tried to convince others of its validity. The more he thought and talked about his dream boat, the more confident he felt of its success as a winner. Consider again his last statement—nothing less than the appealing picture of a lad with an idea affirmed to be of intrinsic value but with no one coming to his rescue, no one willing "to put up the money for the experiment." Then, as though trying to leave behind a dream that refused to come true, he "went West to the Pacific coast." And finally, the anticlimax, "I returned and worked with my Father."

In addition to working in his father's boathouse, Arthur served as yardman for the Burton family, then living in Excelsior on the Dr. Hugh Arey hill. He had to step lively to keep two jobs going, but he was doing still more—he was working overtime in his mental workshop. The increasing desire to put his idea into material form, together with much scheming, planning, and thinking, lent this young man the sober dignity of Socrates himself.

Phillips Brooks once gave this advice to the young men of his day: "Be independent, be courageous, and you will succeed." Fate suddenly decreed that young Dyer should exhibit extreme independence and courage of thought and action. During his days of wishful thinking, he realized that Minnetonka was slipping from the *steamboat* era into that of the *sailboat*. He was on the alert. Would opportunity knock at his door?

Minnetonka Story

For some time previous to the 90's, Excelsior and Wayzata boat builders had been putting out sailing craft of good quality. But imported eastern boats, especially Herreshoff models, were winning all the races on Minnetonka. That was a hard dose for Arthur Dyer to take. His fingers tingled to show the world a real sailboat.

In 1890, the same year that the new yacht clubhouse in St. Louis Bay was completed, Hazen J. Burton, one of the fathers of Minnetonka yachting, bought his Deephaven estate. One day a couple of years later, Mr. Burton and his son Ward sought out young Dyer, still working in his father's boathouse at Excelsior. They brought the news that W. G. Hollis had sent to Herreshoff for his latest 16-foot model. The Burtons wanted a boat to greet Hollis' Herreshoff on its arrival.

Young Dyer's hour had struck; he was ready. Deftly, skillfully, he began work on the Burton order. He worked as calmly and confidently as though it were all "old stuff." Hadn't he already built such a racer a thousand times in his own mind? At last the *Hermes*, a catboat, stood complete. She slipped out alongside the Herreshoff *Coquina* like the veritable goddess of the water she proved to be. Not content to beat the *Coquina* alone, the Burtons' *Hermes* wiped the whole special-class fleet off the slate in the '92 season.

A great victory, but could Arthur Dyer produce a second boat of a winning nature? Roy Wyman answered this question by ordering a Dyer-made cat, the *Kestrel*. Excitement rose to an unbelievable pitch as the *Kestrel* glided out to meet her fate with eastern-made catboats. People were whispering that the *Hermes* was probably just a freak boat; that perhaps mere luck, not skill of construction, accounted for its speed. The *Kestrel* decided the matter when she swept past all rivals in her class.

Thus did Arthur Dyer begin his rise to fame as sailboat designer and builder. To local and eastern builders alike this silent, thoughtful young man was a mystery. He was getting results other builders failed to secure. Other designers went to work armed with the knowledge of mathematics and physics necessary to calculating the centers of effort and resistance. Apparently this designer got along without all the wearisome mathematical work—but how? What was his secret? Was it guesswork or genius?

The element of mystery, added to the hard cold fact of his success, boosted Dyer's stock. The winter of 1893 found him established in his own boat shop on his own island (no longer an island today, however) where the present Deephaven boathouse stands opposite the old Burton home. Orders began to pour in from all quarters; young Dyer had already climbed above local fame.

The '93 yachting season was anticipated with eager interest. Racing hounds, still loyal to eastern builders, stripped their purses for the purchase of new Herreshoffs, while old eastern makes on hand were put in perfect repair. News that the Dyer-made *Apukwa* would appear for the first time in the coming cruise was the red flag—the only signal needed to call every yachtsman to his colors. Upon the appointed day, two hundred and fifty people gathered for the cruise—an arresting spectacle, a typical picture of real sport in the gay 90's.

The nearest we can come to experiencing the actual occasion is by way of a diary written almost sixty years ago by a young Massachusetts girl visiting Minneapolis relatives at that time. In the 90's a girl carried her diary wherever she went and could, without any breach of etiquette, take it out and write anything, anywhere, at any time. On July 22, 1893, the young miss from Massachusetts wrote:

"Hello, little diary! Here we are—Aunt Sadie and I—aboard the *Princess*, out on Lake Minnetonka, pretty much of a pond for a girl used to the ocean! Never went sailing before, except for fun, but this cruise looks like real business. Two hours before starting time, and forty boats already here. Pretty sight—big white-winged birds.

"Most forgot—terribly important, too, just saw Prince Charming near yacht house. My poor heart flutters at the memory! Tall—taller than the other men—broad shoulders—and horribly

good-looking!! All the men were asking him questions. Silent—
eyes on the ground—then he smiled—eyes smiled too—like sunrise at dawn. Hope to meet him. Is he married? Perish the
thought! No, a thousand times *no!*

"Am sixteen today—first real long dress—prettiest one here—
white, figured with red anchors—red sash too. Can't spread out
my train, too many lunch baskets—must hold train in lap—
shucks, no fun! There's the signal—we're off to Mound City—
name sounds good, wonder if it's like Boston. Going to Chapman
House to eat picnic dinner. Woman next to me says a Mr.
Brackett always brings gallons and gallons of baked beans. Could
use some this minute, stomach dancing Yankee Doodle on back-
bone already.

"Sailing, sailing—breeze brisk, sky blue, shores beautiful—
something new every minute, the sweetest white-trunked trees,
the dearest little islands, and millions and millions of birds. Rock-
a-bye, rock-a-bye, slip-slipping, glide-gliding, just about asleep.
Wait a minute, am I seeing a heavenly vision? Can it be? Is that
Prince Charming tending the main sheet of the boat sailing
up alongside ours?

"All awake now. Yes, the Prince! It's the *Volante.* Some of
our passengers are greeting hers: 'Mr. and Mrs. Burton and their
son, Ward,' according to the woman at my right. *Volante* out
of sight, the heavenly vision has passed. Everybody on board
talking about the Burtons and the young men at jib and main
sheet. Little pitchers—big ears! From now on I'm pretending to
be asleep, but I'll be listening just the same. More later!

* * *

"And what did I find out? Young man tending jib—Bob
Shuck. Young man at main sheet—Arthur Dyer—king of my
heart. Prince Charming designs and builds sailboats. This winter he'll have his own island and his own boathouse—like a lord
in his castle. Oh—oh! Follows own original ideas—a genius, already famous. More fame ahead. Goodie, goodie! The more the
better. Asked Aunt Sadie to manage to introduce us, but she
only frowned—horribly homely when she frowns. Answer—

'Impossible, silly!' Plague on it! No fair! Well, the world's still round—may the gods favor our meeting.

"Here we are at Mound City—plenty of mounds but no city. Everybody swarming around my Prince—all but Aunt Sadie, feel like boxing her ears—just contrary, that's all. She thinks she's being proper—anyhow I waved at him behind her back. Wish he'd seen me. Oh, such excitement—air full of congratulations. The Dyer *Apukwa* won by a margin of seventeen minutes. Is my Prince the lion of this occasion? Yes! A courtly, dignified, humble gentleman. Oh, dear—if only Aunt Sadie—well, no matter—back to Massachusetts tomorrow never to hear of him again. Never! Never!"

But she did! Hardly had this young chronicler been home a month before a Boston paper published an article which interested her intensely. She read it over and over and finally hid it away among her keepsakes, only to take it out every now and then to reassure herself of all that the Boston *Herald* of August 30, 1893, told her.

"The *Alpha* beaten! It hardly seemed possible, but later reports from Lake Minnetonka confirm the first report. How was it done? *Alpha*, the little centerboard, won prize after prize in *our* harbor. Now, she has been beaten! Arthur Dyer, the designer of the *Onawa*, has produced a boat of lighter power than the *Alpha*, the Herreshoff 21-footer. Dyer's *Onawa* has a less displacement and a smaller sail plan. In other words the yachtsmen of Minnetonka have a boat that comes nearer to being a canoe than the *Alpha* does.

"It does seem quite a shock to have our best boat beaten by a Westerner. The *Onawa* won over the *Alpha* by a margin of 15 minutes. Our western lakes used to be our best markets for Boston and New York back-numbers, but now! Well, *now* the Minnetonka yachtsmen may claim they have the fastest jib and main sailboat in this country, and for that matter, in the whole world. H. J. Burton owns the *Onawa* and she was sailed by his seventeen-year-old son Ward Burton. The latter will enter Harvard next fall."

Let Arthur Dyer tell you in his own words why and how he built the record-breaking *Onawa*: "One day, along 'bout April, '93, Mr. Burton stepped in at the boathouse—hadn't put up my own shop yet. He looked around to see that nobody was listening—he acted like he wanted to tell me something. Well, he'd found out that E. S. Phelps and Wm. Peet, Jr., were making a trip East—said he had a strong suspicion why they'd gone. Felt pretty sure they were going to look over the fastest sailing craft on the Atlantic seaboard—and buy it at pretty near any cost. What was to be done about it?

"Well, I had the answer. I just pulled out a little model I'd made the year before—all finished even to the varnish—with its specifications tied on it. I told Mr. Burton that I was dead sure a boat made according to that model would be the fastest thing Minnetonka had seen yet. He ordered it on the spot. We talked over the type of construction he preferred and went over the matter of sail area together. From start to finish, everything about this boat was a dead secret.

"Fact is, everything about sailing was kept secret those days. Had a dozen men working for me filling orders, repairing, and one thing or another. You couldn't get a word out of those fellows about their work; no, sir! not for love nor money! They carried on all the other work that spring while I went to work on the Burton boat—the *Onawa*, Mr. Burton named her before she was half done. I enjoyed making that boat the best of any; guess it was my biggest experiment, maybe that's the reason.

"I kept her out of the public eye—when folks came in to give orders or ask for repairs, I just covered her up with a big canvas. How did I make her? Well, not from school books! Rules in books have a pile to say about lateral resistances, centers of buoyancy, centers of effort and gravity, etc. Bosh! I calculate the balance of a boat mostly by my eye; when it looks right, I say it *is* right. You see I'd been thinking out all this myself for years—had pretty definite ideas of my own.

"I built the *Onawa* of cedar, flat ribs laid close, hull and deck covered with light canvas—that canvas sure drunk up a heap of paint. She was firm, no wringing or twisting—easy lines—perfect balance. She was a twenty-one footer, what you call a shallow draught sloop designed to carry a 400-foot sail.

"I said she had perfect balance. Well, maybe that's putting it pretty strong, but the way she acted even on rough water was good to see. Her projecting bow helped keep her in poise. Some said she wasn't much more than just a big canoe. Well, she filled the bill anyhow. Yes, sir, she was a success—a big success if I do say so. Here are some old papers that tell about the races she won. You'll see, she made quite a stir."

And she did. According to the Minneapolis *Journal* of that time:

"Arthur Dyer, the Minnetonka sailboat builder, is famous today. He has succeeded in turning out a craft which is easily the peer of anything in her class in America, a boat which ran right by the famous Herreshoff productions *Alpha* and *Kite* as though they were at anchor."

A few days later from the same paper:

"Arthur Dyer, builder of the now famous sloop *Onawa*, is likely to be in demand with yachtsmen of the East, South and West. New York and Boston papers print column upon column about the *Onawa's* marvellous performances since that wonderful shallow draught sloop was put afloat at Deephaven, and began to win decisive victories over the Herreshoff craft. The fame of *Onawa's* builder, Arthur Dyer, is little less than world wide."

At last, the tables were turned. Not only did local yachtsmen keep their eyes here at home, but eastern enthusiasts turned longing glances westward. Little wonder that eastern yacht clubs felt uneasy—Dyer-made boats were invading their home waters and winning all the laurels with astounding ease. For example, the *Apukwa* (Dyer made) was taken to Massachusetts and straightway won the championship at Marblehead. Then another of his creations, the *Minnetonka*, made the New Yorkers sit up and take notice of the fact that she chalked up three victories in the Larchmont races. Next, the Bostonians received a jolt when the news came that the *Grilse* sent East by Dyer had come off with seven straight victories not far to the south of them, in Buzzard's Bay.

It was always the same gratifying story: a Dyer boat without fail, time after time, in waters fresh or salt, spelled defeat for opponents of any make. A Minneapolis *Times* of 1896 gave Arthur Dyer the following tribute:

139

Minnetonka Story

"All over the world wherever there is a yachting organization or wherever there is an enthusiast anxious to have the fastest boat in his own particular waters, the names of Minnetonka and of Dyer, Minnetonka's boat builder, are known."

The Dyer story is more than the exciting account of record-breaking racing yachts. It is the story of the evolution of an idea: first the small idea of a small boy; then the enlarging idea fed by the streamlined thinking of a growing youth; and at last, the full-fledged idea of a mature young man who came to the realization of success. To be of value, a full-grown idea must be given some sort of expression. That is exactly what happened to Mr. Dyer's idea; to it he gave adequate, corporate form through his own independent, courageous skill. To this man who made his dream come true was rightfully given the title, "Minnetonka's Boat Builder."

CHAPTER XVI | *Days of Sport*

ROWING REGATTAS. We had had a fine visit, Mr. Old-timer and I. He had rambled on delightfully.

"Guess I've told you about everything," he said at last. "No, by Jove! I forgot the best thing yet, the rowing races that began in the 80's. Whenever there was a 'shell race,' as we kids called it, we had ringside seats up in the trees around Gideon's Bay. The race course ran across the bay from Excelsior to Lake Park Hotel.

"There was always big excitement when the contesting teams with their own shells began coming from Duluth, Lake Pepin, Lake Geneva, Winnipeg, and Lake Winnebago. Thousands of rooters trailed after their teams—and so did we kids.

"But the day of the race, well, sir! that was something to remember. Hours before the race was to start, the shore began filling up with carriages and lumber wagons loaded with folks. Everything that could float, from rafts to steamboats, lined up along the race course. Folks on board and on shore began to sing and wave little flags they'd brought. Lake Park's verandas waved and sang in answer—sounded real pretty.

"If there's anything more thrilling than trained oarsmen, wearing their bright crew shirts, waiting at attention for the go-signal —well! I wouldn't know what it is, unless it's the race itself.

"To see the crews work with machine-like precision; to watch the oars rise and fall without wavering a hair's breadth; to see each shell slice the water leaving its wake to fan out behind— ah, such a sight! It's a wonder every last one of us kids didn't fall of his perch.

141

Minnetonka Story

"Toward the end of the race everybody got still's death. When one of the shells the last minute shot ahead like a meteor, the crowd went wild. Steamboats whistled and rang their bells, and bands began to play like all possessed.

"By the time I got me long pants and a girl, Cornell and Harvard had decided on the Upper Lake for their shell race. The course was charted from Halstead's Pass to Woodside, where R. O. Foster lives now.

"On Enchanted Island, about two-thirds of the way from the starting point, bleachers were put up for spectators. My girl and I sat in the top row with a bag of peanuts and a pocketful of candy hearts. It was my first date and I wasn't paying much attention to the race when it began, but as the shells passed us, the Harvard crew got a slight bulge on Cornell. 'Pon my word it was a great sight. The crowd yelled itself hoarse, encouraging the crews. One old Harvard rooter got so excited, he fainted dead away. When all the steamers turned and followed a long ways behind, we knew they wanted to be on hand at the finish."

"And who won?" I asked.

"Well, now," he pondered, "I don't rightly remember. Guess 'twas Harvard that time."

Everett Mann, of Mound, offered this information about rowing regattas: "Shell races on Lake Minnetonka continued from the 80's until recently. Duluth, Winnipeg, Fort William, and Port Arthur were always eager to compete with a Minneapolis or St. Paul team.

"A shell race is worth seeing whether the crews are made up of two, four, or eight men. An eight-man crew has a coxswain who gets a good ducking in the lake when his team wins.

"A contest between Fort William and St. Paul on July 20, 1935, was the last shell race on our lake."

ICEBOATING. Excelsior had the first iceboat fleet—fifteen to twenty boats with Leroy Sampson acting as commodore. At first, any boat carrying the correct sail spread would do. Only two men were needed, one for each sail, but sociable Mr. Sampson filled his boat to capacity with passengers. For them it was a hair-raising experience to shoot across a sheet of glass and find themselves in Wayzata almost before they had started.

The iceboat clubhouse, built in 1900 on a small island near the yacht clubhouse, was an attractive, hospitable establishment designed for entertaining. Every Saturday, if conditions were favorable, was devoted to iceboat racing. The course was set from Deephaven to Wayzata and back.

A large shipment of iceboats came from the Hudson River in the late 80's, among which were the *Reindeer* and the *St. Nicholas*, former champions on the Hudson. The *St. Nicholas* continued to outrun all rivals. These beautiful boats gave ice yachting on Minnetonka a wonderful impetus. Contesting teams came from the Hudson River, Lake Michigan, Lake Superior, Fort William, and Port Arthur.

Alf Pillsbury and Al Loring were the moving spirits in the latter days of iceboating, inscribing their names indelibly upon this particular brand of Minnetonka sports. According to the Minnetonka *Record*: "The Hudson Cup which is open to United States competition, also the Northwest Pennant of America have been won by our iceboat club during this season of 1899 and 1900—after five of our best winters for iceboating."

After each regatta on our lake, the visitors were entertained in our iceboat clubhouse, which was operated by a colored couple, the Woodfords. Guests were glad to exchange the bitter cold outside for the warm comfort of the clubhouse, where steaming food and fragrant coffee had been prepared by Mr. Woodford, an ex-Pullman chef.

TENNIS. To the people of this recently settled Northwest, the game of lawn tennis may have seemed novel, but it was not new. Tennis, history assures us, was the game of kings, princes, knights, nobles, and aristocrats as far back as the year 1316. A game of kings it may have been, but it has become the king of games in the hands of English, Australian, and American stars.

The Minneapolis *Journal* publicized the growing popularity of tennis in the East, recommending it as a graceful game for young women, also. At the same time, it described a lady's attire suitable for a game on the court as follows: "A tennis dress should have sleeves puffed at the shoulder. It may be had at a low figure if one makes it herself, using striped outing flannel which is very pretty and costs around 12 cents a yard. Pink and grey is a good combination with grey stockings, tennis shoes laced with scarlet, a scarlet tam o' shanter and a large silk sash also scarlet."

The first Northwest Tournament was held in the late summer of 1890 on the Hamline University courts. For the next few years, this tournament made the rounds of the big hotels: Hotel Lafayette, Hotel St. Louis, Lake Park Hotel, etc.—wherever first-class courts were provided. In 1891, the following notice appeared in the *Northwest Tourist*: "The Northwest Tennis Tournament will be held at Hotel St. Louis. The northwestern cracks will be there. Trafford Jayne and George Belden will meet and decide honors. It is expected that Belden and Wallace will be pitted against Jayne and Thorne. The Hotel St. Louis management has offered $250 in prizes."

As the gay 90's neared the turn of the century, the Minnetonka picture began losing its highlights: its steamboats with their gay clientele, its hotels with their fine tennis courts. Our lake finally realized that "old things are passed away." The Northwest Tournament, however, was not an old thing. It was still new, still very young—all dressed up, looking for a place to go.

On the Deephaven Burton estate there is a natural amphitheater formed by hills on three sides with the lake on the fourth. When the Burton family invited the homeless tournament into this place, obviously prepared by Nature for such an event, the invitation was accepted. From 1901 until the world went to war in 1939, Northwest Tournaments were held on the Burton courts without interruption.

Mrs. Burton and her daughters, Hazel and Ariel, were most gracious hostesses. Guests from farthest away were entertained at the Burton home, besides twenty or thirty extras at lunch. On the Burton table there was honest-to-goodness food: baked beans, home-made bread, beef, fried chicken, vegetables, berries, milk, cream, butter, and cottage cheese quite yellow with cream.

(Mrs. Burton gave personal attention to her dairy products.) Such fare her vistors never forgot.

One day as the guests hurried up the path to the Burton home, a priest took note of their destination. This priest was a stranger; not to tennis, but to this locality. (Back in divinity college days he had been a tennis champion, so he had followed the tournament out here.) Now, as mealtime approached, he naturally went along to the hotel with the others—at least, that is what he thought the Burton house must be. He sat down to rest hoping to make the second table. When nothing happened, he knocked at the door and asked when the next meal was to be served. With true New England dignity, softened by kindly courtesy, Mrs. Burton explained matters. Then she insisted on giving the stranger at her door a hearty meal. As the priest rose to leave, he blessed the kindness of his hostess.

The Northwest Tournament continued to bring great throngs to the Burton courts. Crowds of gaily dressed spectators, perching on the hillsides, flung vivid colors against the green background of the woodland. It was a brilliant picture. The games in the valley below added the brilliancy of grace, speed, alertness, quick wit, and perfect coordination of mind and muscle.

Once during a tournament a man near us explained to his son why he thought tennis was the best of games: "You see, my boy, there is always something *new* in tennis. The variety of strokes is amazing; the variety of courts is also to be considered. If you've got the right sort of a tennis brain, you'll find the tennis ball just heavy enough, just solid enough to keep you busy combining all the skill and strength and control you can muster. Besides, you've got to discover the other fellow's weakness and capitalize on that. Tire him out at his weak spot. Son, do you want to know who's got tennis brains? Johnston and McLaughlin have."

Many tennis fans will recall when these two Californians faced each other at Forest Hills, New York—twenty-year-old William Johnston, a 115 pounder vs. Maurice McLaughlin, older, and heavier. Seven thousand spectators that day realized how

Johnston, discovering that McLaughlin's power lay close to the net, played his opponent deep. Here lay victory for Johnston.

These great stars have played on the Burton courts, as have Tom Bunday, Reuben Hunt, Ray Little, and others. The long list of local tennis stars, whose wives grow weary of shining their trophies, begins with George Belden, Trafford Jayne, Harry Waidner, John Adams, Jr., Henry Norton, Henry Adams, Joe Armstrong, Lauren Kennedy, Seifert Stellwagon, Dr. Widen, and Ward Burton playing doubles with his son Gale.

There can be little doubt that the hundreds of spectators who sat year after year upon the Burton hills, witnessing the remarkable performances of singles, doubles, and mixed doubles, returned to their homes each time with a new zest for this great game. Their own courts received a thorough going-over, and even youngsters began practicing the new strokes. The Northwest Tournaments, like sailing and rowing regattas and iceboat races, linked Minnetonka to the outside world of sports.

CHAPTER XVII

Minnetonka's Fruit Basket

WHEN Minnetonka's honeymoon was over and her days of pomp had passed into days of circumstance, she still held in her grasp two elements of enduring fame: sailing and fruit growing. Lake Minnetonka herself continues to be the sailor's delight while her countryside claims the glory of being the birthplace of the Wealthy and Haralson apples, the Latham raspberry, the Red Lake currant, the Underwood and other plums.

If it is correct that America has 1,000 distinct varieties of apples, Minnetonkans could manage without 998 of them, provided they were amply supplied with the two kinds of apples that have made their region famous—the Wealthy and the Haralson.

Minnesota's early settlers had a fruit tooth. Fortunately wild berries, grapes, plums, and chokecherries grew in abundance. Apples? Well, apples belonged "back home." The very word called up memories of cider, apple pies, mincemeat, applesauce, and barrels of fragrant apples in the cellar for winter.

Such memories stirred the heart of St. Anthony's Rev. Gideon Pond when a dozen apple seeds fell out of a letter from his old New England home. Slyly, almost furtively, he planted them. As his seedlings grew, his hopes mounted.

Nobody knows exactly when Preacher Pond picked the first apple crop ever raised in Minnesota. Perhaps it was in the late 40's that hungry pioneers crowded around to get a look at the little sour yellow apples from his seedlings.

"Maybe they taste better than they look," somebody suggested hopefully, but they didn't.

"Wheat's the stuff to raise here," commented another. "Looks

like apples are no go for Minnesota; too blame near the North
Pole."

Ever since the Rev. Gideon Pond had come west as missionary
to the Indians, he had longed for applesauce. After he had planted his apple seeds, he had had to wait long years for results—
but such results!

Swallowing his disappointment, Missionary Pond decided it
was easier to convert the Indians than to raise apples in Minnesota, so he put applesauce out of his mind and pressed on toward
the mark of his high calling.

* * *

Some years later, in '53, an apple-minded man joined the Excelsior colony. With commendable apple sense, Peter Gideon chose
the 160-acre claim skirting the bay that now bears his name—
that bay would help keep away late spring frosts. There is a
huge rock bearing a written memorial to Minnesota's first successful orchardist on the site of his claim, located to the left of
the track at Manitou on the way from Excelsior to Wildhurst.

In his diary, Robert McGrath records his first meeting with
Peter Gideon, "an apple-crazy man, crazy even to imagine apple
trees can stand such a frigid climate as this." He told Peter what
a flop Preacher Pond's apples had proved to be. Minnesota was
never meant for apples, that was certain. But Peter only laughed
and said, "Wait and see!"

Robert did wait for twenty years and more. Then one day
he saw the impossible hanging from Peter's trees. "Well, Peter,
you've done it," he admitted. "What are you calling it?"

"My wife's name is Wealthy. That's a good enough name for
my apple," was Peter's reply.

Peter Gideon's method was the seedling way—which consisted
of planting the apple seeds, caring for the delicate little apple
plants, transplanting them into nursery rows, and later spacing
them far enough apart to insure a sturdy growth. When these
seedlings finally came into bearing, he propagated the choicest
ones by the use of scions, which are twigs taken from the de-
sirable seedlings and grafted onto the roots of some hardy variety

of apple. Mr. Gideon often used the root system of the Russian crab for this purpose. In time the scion becomes a tree bearing the same kind of fruit as its parent.

Mr. Gideon kept on year after year planting more and still more seeds. He reasoned that apples which could thrive in Maine, with the same latitude as Minnesota, would be apt to resist the rigors of our climate. For many years he secured seeds through his trusted friend, Albert Emerson, of Bangor, Maine.

By the fall of 1862, the Gideon orchards were good to look upon. The following summer, however, brought a distressing drought. Whatever trees survived that summer's heat fell victim to the following winter's merciless cold. Ten years' work was wiped out with not a tree left. Even his bay was leaving him, for every day the water level was lower. Times were hard, money was scarce. Mr. Gideon had only enough cash on hand for a suit of clothes. He needed the clothes, but he wanted apple seeds worse. Springtime found Mr. Gideon precariously clad in a suit tailored from two vests and an old pair of trousers, but exuberantly happy as he planted a new orchard.

Records are vague as to the exact year that the Wealthy apple came into existence and stood all the tests necessary for a Minnesota apple to meet. Before 1878, however, the Wealthy was pronounced the best apple as yet produced in the Middle West. It has since made wealthy many a Wisconsin, Minnesota, and Iowa fruit grower.

As a result of Mr. Gideon's success with the Wealthy apple, our state legislature bought a strip of land adjoining his homestead and offered him this land and a salary of $1,000 a year to assist him to even greater accomplishments. This arrangement seems to have continued for ten years or so.

Peter Gideon owned and operated an alert mind; he was continually reaching out for new conquests. For instance, he raised bushels of rosy-cheeked peaches, the Ohio and Michigan kind, according to Mr. Becker, of Tonka Bay.

This is the method Mr. Gideon used: every fall he cut the roots on one side of the peach trees, then bent the trees to the ground in the opposite direction and covered them with straw and dirt. Neatly tucked away, those peach trees escaped winter hardships. In the spring they were helped out of their snug beds and tied to stakes. By autumn every tree hung full of peaches.

To this day, on the Gideon homestead, there survive mute witnesses to the outreaching ambitions of its pioneer owner: groves of shellbark hickory nuts and walnuts, outcroppings of strange, foreign-looking shrubs, besides patches of queer looking green grapes draping the sumach bushes that have stolen the once well-kept vineyard.

Peter Gideon's acres were, in those days, the state's A-No. 1 show place. Almost every day Minneapolis and St. Paul residents hitched up and drove out to marvel at Peter's bridal wreath, the first in the state. Long peony beds, clumps of Russian golden willow, and rows of apple trees, bursting into pink, fringed the blue of his nearby bay.

In the midst of all this loveliness, Peter Gideon was a solitary figure. He was surrounded by his family (a wife and six children); he was visited and honored by countless friends; he was courted and esteemed by horticulturists of surrounding states —and yet, Peter Gideon was alone. He was a recluse within his own soul. As a spiritualist, he could leave this world and visit "sin's hole" at the center of our earth, where he found new strength to live.

Spiritualism gave Peter Gideon's soul an uplift; it saved him time and money besides. If his cows lost their way in the Big Woods, he held his hands over his head, followed the leading, and there were his cows. No time lost! If any of the family fell ill, no doctor was needed. Peter believed in the "laying on of hands," and the ailing one recovered. No money spent! This meant time and money saved for fruit breeding projects.

During the last years before his death in 1899, Peter Gideon preferred to dwell alone. He sent his wife, Wealthy, to live with one of their children. Today not one of his family survives, but his Wealthy apple still thrives.

* * *

Some room in Minnetonka's fruit basket should be given to grapes. In 1883, Minnetonka won the blue ribbon at the United States Pomological Association Exhibit held in Philadelphia. In 1885, grapes entered from the Minnetonka region won first prize at the New Orleans Exposition. Five years later, the Minneapolis *Journal* stated: "60,000 pounds of grapes from Minnetonka are shipped annually, after fully supplying the Twin Cities."

Mr. Reel, the only living exponent of a once-thriving grape culture in this locality, was glad to write of his success along that line.

"Not far from Christmas Lake," he wrote, "A. W. Latham operated a nursery in which he propagated nursery stock from eastern varieties of grapes. He never originated any new variety.

"I often visited that nursery when I first came to Minnetonka. Due to Mr. Latham's encouragement, I put in my 'White Crows' vineyard of 4,000 vines near Christmas Lake. I sprayed my grapes with Bordeau as early as 1890, and it paid. For twelve years I exhibited my grapes at the State Fair taking 130 first prizes, 32 seconds, and 14 thirds.

"When grapes were shipped in from the East, prices fell and I dug up my vines. The large vineyards near the present Vine Hill station were dug up, too, but the terraces on the hillsides can still be seen. On my new place, Dixie Orchard, I raised thirty-four varieties of grapes."

* * *

Some years ago, one of Minnesota's greatest fruit breeders brought his family to our neighborhood to live. Charles Haralson's appearance and bearing suggested solid determination and firm decision. He was calm, self-contained and reserved, and yet he liked fun—a good story sent him off into hearty laughter.

We often wondered if he had had his full share of fun and nonsense back in Sweden. His voice always took on a wistful note when he mentioned his boyhood in the little hamlet of Jareda. At sixteen, Charles found himself in America, a strange country with a strange language. He became a loyal American citizen and learned to use a clear, careful, forceful English.

While at work in the Rose Hill nursery, young Haralson had decided that his life work should be devoted to plants and fruit trees. Then a call came from the South Dakota State College of Agriculture at Brookings. Dr. Niels E. Hansen, the greatest living plant breeder, needed an assistant. He had traveled through Russia, China, and northern European countries, gathering hardy grasses, plants, and fruits which could be crossed with more tender varieties here in America, so that the resulting plants and fruits might bear up under our severe northern climate.

Charles Haralson's first job at Brookings was to take a camel's-hair brush and hand pollinate the blossoms on the tubbed apple trees just then being forced into bloom in the college green-houses. "That brush looked pretty small to me," he used to say, "and so did the grains of pollen to be transferred from blossom to blossom. But there wasn't anything small about my hands— they're plenty big, worse luck!

"Well, sir, I took a long breath and went at that job as if life depended on it, and I got along first-class. I kept track of the seedling apples from that first fruit breeding job of mine, and such devilish poor specimens you never saw! Fruit breeding belongs to the world of beginning again—I had learned that much, anyhow.

"Once I told Dr. Hansen I intended to develop a large red winter apple for the Dakotas and Minnesota. 'We need such an apple,' he agreed. 'It's a big dream, but go to it!' "

And that is exactly what Charles Haralson did when he be-came superintendent of the Minnesota University Fruit Breed-ing Farm at Zumbra Heights in 1907. Now, entirely on his own, Mr. Haralson turned his attention to what Dr. Hansen had styled "a big dream." This dream had to come true.

As in his Brookings job, the first step was the hand pollination of choice young apple trees forced into bloom in greenhouses. Thousands of seeds from the resulting apples were planted and the seedlings nursed along until they should come into bearing. Sometimes Mr. Haralson sent for scions of eastern and mid-western varieties of apples to graft onto tubbed trees, thereby producing new supplies of pollen for new strains.

Fruit breeding is a continuous process: pollen, seeds, then thousands of seedlings to be labeled. The long-awaited fruit is generally unsatisfactory, a poor reward for the fruit breeder's unremitting labor. That means he must begin over again, year after year, until successful.

After ten years of such labor, Mr. Haralson held his dream apple in his hand. Then came a long series of rigid tests before the new apple could be accepted by horticulturists. Having passed all tests with flying colors, the Haralson apple was ready to be propagated either by budding or grafting.

The Haralson apple is red, large, well-shaped, and delicious. It is a remarkable eater, cooker, and keeper; in fact, it will keep a year if stored properly. It never disappoints. It is an increasing source of wealth to the commercial grower and a great delight to the home owner who has room for only a few trees in his back yard.

At first thought it would seem less exacting to develop new varieties of apples and plums, easier than to work with currants and raspberries, which have tiny seeds and delicate seedlings almost too small to handle. Mr. Haralson, however, made no such discrimination. While developing his famous Haralson apple, he produced other varieties, including the Wedge and the President Folwell. Among the plums he originated, favorites include the Underwood, Elliott, Monitor, and Juanita.

All this time he was working on currants and raspberries. At last, he realized success in the Red Lake currant and the Latham raspberry. Note that it is Charles Haralson who originated the Latham raspberry, which he named in honor of one of Minnesota's early fruit growers, A. W. Latham.

The Latham raspberry, sometimes called Minnesota No. 4, is the most widely planted variety of red raspberry in the United States and Canada. There is good reason: it is large, delicious, prolific, and hardy. It is a highly valued commercial berry, and equally satisfactory in a small back yard.

How Mr. Haralson accomplished such a prodigious amount of work is past understanding. He kept from fifteen to seventeen men on the experimental farm at Zumbra Heights, but his son Elmer was his father's sole helper in the fruit-breeding job. "Elmer could be trusted," explained his father. "It is such exacting work that one false or thoughtless move could easily undo the work of years."

As long as Samuel B. Greene of our State University horticultural department lived, he was proud of himself for having called Charles Haralson back to Minnesota's Fruit Breeding Farm after he had been so splendidly trained by Dr. Hansen in the South Dakota experimental station.

Wondering if Dr. Niels Hansen, now long past eighty, still remembered Mr. Haralson, I wrote him. Here is the Doctor's reply: "Do I remember Charles Haralson? Yes! He worked as foreman here in our agricultural experiment station for eight years. I taught him fruit breeding. He was very efficient. He deserves great credit for his work both in South Dakota and Minnesota. His Haralson apple and Latham raspberry are of the highest quality."

Mr. Haralson retired in 1924. Fifteen years later he was presented with a plaque by the State Nursery Association in honor of his "outstanding creative work in horticulture." He enjoyed this visible proof of his fellow workers' esteem and appreciation the two years remaining before his death.

Charles Haralson proved the truth of Dr. Hansen's tribute "very efficient." He used head and hand with preeminent success in his chosen field. At last, he came forward with offerings of rare beauty and great value to place beside Peter Gideon's Wealthy in Minnetonka's fruit basket.

CHAPTER XVIII | *Do You Know Minnetonka?*

How often I heard "By the Waters of Minnetonka" pouring from bus station and airport juke boxes during my visits in the South, I cannot say. Almost always the majority of the travelers, who had given little heed to previous records, began to listen to the rippling of the waves and the longings of the human heart expressed in that pensive melody. One time a pretty WAC near me gave such a tremulous sigh that I asked by way of sympathy, "Where is Minnetonka?"

She gave me a sad look, grieved at my ignorance. "Oh, it isn't anywhere. It's just an imaginary place, sort of a Shangri-La, you know."

In a way she was right. Minnetonka is a sort of Shangri-La where Nature offers concentrated beauty of lake and shore and surrounding terrain, a spot where youth lingers and old age is loath to appear.

Have you ever seen this Shangri-La from the air? Many years ago a neighbor boy, Harry Holcomb, flew our family over the lake. From above it looks like a huge octopus twisting its arms in all directions. Its hundred miles of shoreline form a confusing cat's cradle of bays and peninsulas trimmed in birch, cedar, elm, oak and maple—all second growth except on Halstead's Bay and on the R. M. Bennett estate where a few gigantic maples remain as primitive reminders of the Big Woods. Its islands are all sizes from neat little one-house Gale Island to sprawling town-sized Phelps Island.

Suspended over our lake in Harry's little eggshell, we had time to imagine how Minnetonka looked wearing her belt of Indian teepees and bright campfires followed by a girdle of little pioneer towns, drab and cheerless until Minnetonka's golden age brightened them up with gay hotels and luxurious steamboats. As we looked down, we realized she had put on a new belt, a belt of summer homes and cottages, interspersed with occasional winter homes.

Recently we saw our lake again from a plane. Now she is wearing a widely expanding belt of year-round homes which, viewed from above, seem to be caught in an amazing network of ribbon-like roads. We were given a passing glance at Minnetonka's towns and settlements studded with large modern schoolhouses and punctuated with shining church spires. Our lake that morning looked like a rich blue sapphire set in the green-gold of spring foliage.

Those who know Minnetonka regard her with affection. Dr. T. C. Blegen, dean of the University graduate school, confesses he has loved this lake ever since his boyhood days spent on Saga Hill.

James Ford Bell, President of General Mills, Inc., made his first trip to the old Lafayette in 1889 and has been going there ever since. He says:

"It is delightful to hasten from the clamor and noise of the city and of the business world to Minnetonka's peaceful shores, where one renews his strength for the problems of tomorrow."

When Governor Luther W. Youngdahl was asked how he happened to build in this locality, he answered:

"I particularly like the friendliness and neighborliness of the people of Minnetonka and the lake region. Then, too, I have known and loved the beauty and serenity of Lake Minnetonka since childhood and have long looked forward to the day when I could build a home on its shores."

Minnetonkans enjoy a variety of pleasant activities. Sailing since the war has again come into great favor, and the number of cruisers, houseboats, and other water craft is increasing. In fact, Archie Cochrane of Cochranes' Boat Yard estimates that there are between forty and fifty kinds of water vehicles on the lake, from handsome cruisers like the one owned by Cedric Adams down to contraptions rigged up by the neighbor boys.

Sailors and landlubbers alike are proud of the new yacht club-house at Deephaven which replaces the old one recently destroyed by fire.

Those who prefer land to water have other diversions. Some spend quiet hours in their flower gardens, restocking and re-arranging, the better to welcome garden club tours. Others are content with old-fashioned, fool-proof flower beds where dogs kick up the petunias and roll on the marigolds before digging out a cool bed for themselves under the hollyhocks.

Some people keep fit by playing tennis or golf or by cantering along our country roads. Those seriously devoted to horsemanship look upon the Woodhill Horse Show in late July as the highlight of the season. In early spring, junior and senior horsemen begin training along forty-miles of cross-country trails where jumps over pasture fences have been provided.

To sportsmen this lake means fishing. According to John B. Moyle, Aquatic Biologist of the Minnesota Conservation Department:

"The game fish population of Lake Minnetonka is as large and as good as in most lakes in northern Minnesota. Fifteen kinds of edible fish populate this lake. In 1949, we found twice as many northern pike per acre as in the average Minnesota lake, and their weight was a third above the state-wide average."

Many Minnetonkans go hiking or birding. The late Dr. Thomas S. Roberts called this region his bird paradise. In fact, he claimed he got his start in ornithology the day Skipper Galpin took him aboard the *Governor Ramsey* to see a flock of rare sandpipers on Big Island. That was when Dr. Roberts was a little boy, but Minnetonka is still the center of a thriving bird population.

When summer birds have gone and the trees are bare, when the late fall winds moan like the lost soul of Judas Iscariot and the lake begins to flirt with King Boreas and at last stiffens in his embrace—winter has come. Like a tired child too sleepy to see winter's show through, this lakeside always seems glad to snuggle down under a coverlet of snow.

Minnetonka Story

When year-round homes were first established in this area, it was the winter months that seemed to weld the family together. Life at Minnetonka has from the beginning placed emphasis upon the family. The pioneer family cleared the new claim. It was the family that went ginsenging, the family that ran the boarding house. When Minnetonka's golden age arrived, guests came for the season with their families.

Nowadays winter at Minnetonka still means family fun indoors and out with games, music, and reading or tobogganing, skiing and skating. Before the children grow up they have had many winters to enjoy with Dad and Mom these activities which have made the family circle a reality in their lives.

When the children have finally left home, Dad and Mom still keep the home fires burning. They are reaching "the last of life for which the first was made." Before the fire they read or chat or think aloud, trying to keep up with the march of time. Home life here seldom bogs down.

If you know Minnetonka in winter, you know a place where crystal-clear air allows undimmed splendor of sunrise and sunset; a place where Jack Frost undisturbed spreads his mantle of fairy lacework while moonlight glorifies a white world with glistening silver.

If you know Minnetonka in summer, you know a place where the bittersweet grows and the birds sing all the day long; a place where the sun shines yellow as gold, and the apple trees burst with pink-tinged snow. If you know Minnetonka, you know a place where life is good.

The year 1953 will mark the end of this region's first hundred years lived as a part of the civilized world. For Minnetonka to exchange the red man's campground for the white man's Shangri-La, a century has been none too long.

Illustrations

2. *Charles Galpin*
—Minnetonka's
Miracle Man—
preacher
teacher
skipper
tinsmith
surveyor
mailman
dentist

3. *Trinity Episcopal Church, Excelsior, when surrounded*
   by stockade during the Indian Massacre of '62

4. *Lake View, one of the oldest hotels on Upper Lake*

5. *Lake Park Hotel on Gideon's Bay, the first big hotel*

6. *Hotel Lafayette built by James J. Hill between the Upper and Lower Lakes*

7. *Hotel St. Louis, Deephaven, built by Sir Charles Gibson*

8. *The White House, built at Excelsior in '72, one of the last hotels to go out of business*

9. *Guests who returned year after year to the White House*

10. *The Sue Gardiner, Lake Minnetonka's second steamboat*

11. *The Belle of Minnetonka*

12. *The City of St. Louis*

13. *Crystal Bay,* one of Minnetonka's loveliest coves

14. *Captain
Frank Halstead,
the younger
hermit*

15. *Major
George Halstead
at home*

16. *The Minnetonka Mill and adjacent buildings*

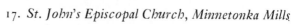

17. *St. John's Episcopal Church, Minnetonka Mills*

18. *Mary Burwell,
the bride
at the Mills*

19. *John R. Johnson,
Minnetonka's Sea Dog,
at 25 years of age*

20. *Arthur Dyer, at 20,*
Minnetonka's Boat Builder

21. *Peter Gideon,*
originator of the Wealthy apple

22. *Charles Haralson developed the apple which bears his name*

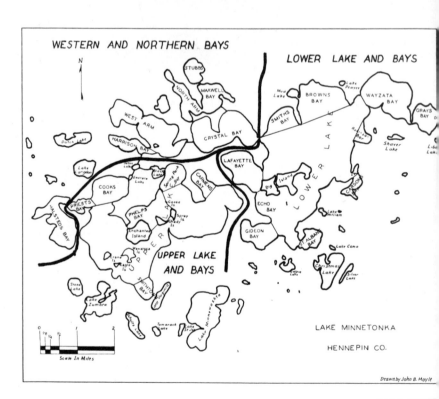